Country Towns of

MAINE

Charming Small Towns and
Villages to Explore

Donna Gold

D1206463

COUNTRY ROADS PRESS
NTC/Contemporary Publishing Group

Library of Congress Cataloging-in-Publication Data

Gold, Donna, 1953–
    Country towns of Maine : charming small towns and villages to
explore / Donna Gold.
       p.   cm. — (Country towns)
    Includes bibliographical references.
    ISBN 1-56626-194-5
    1. Maine—Guidebooks.   2. Cities and towns—Maine—Guidebooks.
I. Title.   II. Series.
F17.3.G66   1998
917.4104'43—dc21   98-39697
                                                    CIP

Excerpt on p. 20, from *Newfield, Maine: The First 200 Years*, is reprinted by
permission of the Board of Selectmen of Newfield, Maine.

Excerpt on p. 49, from "Can World of Christina Be Saved?" by Bill Caldwell,
originally published in the *Portland Sunday Telegram*, June 1, 1969, is reprinted
by permission of The Portland Newspapers.

Excerpt on pp. 95–96, from "The Grand Adventure," by Philmore Wass, is
reprinted by permission of *Down East Magazine*.

Excerpts from John Marin's letters, pp. 100 and 101, are from *John Marin*,
edited by Cleve Gray, © 1977 by Cleve Gray. Reprinted by permission of Henry
Holt and Company, Inc.

Cover and interior design by Nick Panos
Cover and interior illustrations and map copyright © Kathleen O'Malley

Published by Country Roads Press
A division of NTC/Contemporary Publishing Group, Inc.
4255 West Touhy Avenue, Lincolnwood (Chicago), Illinois 60646-1975 U.S.A.
Copyright © 1999 by Donna Gold
Manufactured in the United States of America
International Standard Book Number: 1-56626-194-5
98 99 00 01 02 03 ML 18 17 16 15 14 13 12 11 10 9 8 7 6 5 4 3 2 1

For my parents, Judy and Irving, and for my brother, Ron,
sharers in my earliest travels

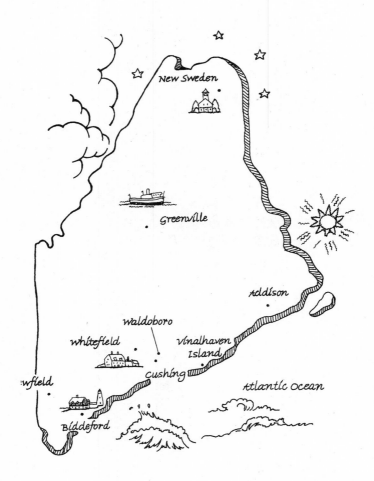

CONTENTS

PREFACE

The first I ever knew of Maine was as a child of nine when I was put on a train and sent here to summer camp. I was not happy to be going. I was a shy child, a reader, not an athlete, and this camp was very much about sports. As for hikes, I had never been on one. At the end of the summer, while friends proudly got trophies and titles, I got the camp booby prize: my name permanently engraved on a plaque as "most improved." The plaque may still hang in the camp dining room, for all I know. I haven't been back to see.

But something grew within my discomfort and loneliness. Twenty years later, when my thrill for urban adventure had turned to a craving for peace, I found myself longing for the shelter of a forest, for the soft feel of moss and the smell of pine. I bought a car—my first—and drove north. When I stopped, I was in Maine. That was fourteen years and five cars ago. I've been driving around this great state ever since.

What follows are some of my explorations. Think of these chapters as impressionistic portraits, not deep histories, following one of my favorite sayings: Only as a tourist do you truly know a place. When I enter a town as a visitor, my eyes are wide, my mind fresh, I can make connections without critiques. And while I may come to know the place better, I will never again see it as clearly. I have tried to stay with my first impressions here, buoyed up by some background, some sense of how things got this way.

Expect to find conversations and some reason to get out of the car—a canoe trip, a museum, a store, a hike, even a tour of roadside utility poles. Expect also to find some regional history, because in Maine, history is palpable. Stand by the coast in Cushing, or out on Vinalhaven. A schooner crosses the horizon, sails unfurled like angel wings. It's as if the nineteenth century were still around. There are places in Maine where you can walk a dirt road and still hear the clopping of hooves; there are rivers and lakes through which you can canoe and be so alone you might imagine yourself as an early explorer, or as a member of a Wabanaki tribe. Maine has a lot of space and not many people; a lot of the old ways remain.

And just as the era of cellphones, E-mail, and the Internet had threatened to take the place of community, the ice storm of 1998 cut power to much of Maine for nearly two weeks. Hauling buckets of water over the ice, lighting my way to the kitchen by candle, stoking the wood stove to snake heat to back rooms, I had a lot of time to question my interest in the old days. After twelve days of darkness, I was thankful to be so affected by weather. This balance of protection and vulnerability we live within keeps us aware. It matters, deeply, whether it's sunny or cloudy, hot or cold, icy or snowy, especially if we are relying on daylight for sight, on rainfall for drink and on ambient temperature for heat. In heating old weathered homes with wood, in checking in on neighbors, in lending a hand, we connected to the center of being—to how we as a people, as a community, and as a nation were formed.

Anyone who knows Maine will find my choice of towns unusual, if not downright obscure. I have deliberately picked towns that are off the tourist track. You won't find Camden here, or Boothbay or Bar Harbor. Yet many of the towns I cover have spent some times as tourist destinations—Greenville has been a popular spot to visit for over a century, Cushing has had its share of visitors, and Waldoboro's Moody's Diner is still a stopping place for many.

What I am offering here are towns that represent an older Maine, before the 1980s and '90s slicked things up. When you visit a house, you don't want to be limited to the porch swing, or a spruced-up living room, do you? You want to know the secrets. Don't you try to sneak a peek at the kitchen, the bedroom, the barn—the private spaces where life is strongest?

The towns in this book all have lovely porches—and also some way of accessing the inner Maine.

Don't forget *The Maine Atlas & Gazetteer*, published by DeLorme Mapping. It provides the best guide to back roads, those that lead to the small, essential parts of Maine—roads that most maps ignore. And remember, there may not always be places to stay or eat in each town, so plan accordingly.

ACKNOWLEDGMENTS

Thanks to all those who helped me in this endeavor, especially to my readers: Herb Adams, Steve Cartwright, Elaine Crossman, Janice Kasper, Natasha Mayers, Barbara O'Brien, John Oddy, Mabel Todd, Joan Yeaton, and, of course, Bill Carpenter. You have steered me away from some grievous errors. I hope that I have not added other ones during subsequent edits. If I have, please tell me what they are.

Thanks also go to the encouragement and savvy of the editors at the various newspapers for which I have written. Some portions of some chapters may have appeared in similar forms in the following newspapers: *Boston Globe, Kennebec Journal, Lewiston Sun Journal, Maine Times,* and *Portland Press Herald.*

More thanks go to my local libraries—the Belfast Free Library, the Buck Memorial Library in Bucksport, Augusta's Maine State Library, and the Thorndike Library at College of the Atlantic in Bar Harbor. Your books cultivated towers throughout the house I share with my family, Bill and Daniel, who once again kindly put up with my long hours and papery messes.

Finally, thanks to the people in every town who have given of their stories and their time, and have borne up under my numerous, un-Yankeelike questions.

1
BIRDING
BIDDEFORD POOL

(STATE ROUTE 208, 8 MILES SOUTHEAST
OF BIDDEFORD, 10 MILES NORTHEAST
OF KENNEBUNKPORT)

From off the headlands of the Kennebunks, a point sweeps out to sea in an almost dizzying gesture. Biddeford Pool is the name given to this land where at high tide the head and neck of it trap a "pool"—a mile-wide body of water that, except for the dredged harbor, empties to a marshy mudflat at low tide.

As a small fishing village with a great harbor, Biddeford Pool is defined by its geography. Each spring and fall, thousands of birds flock to the feeding grounds of the Pool on their annual migrations. In summer, city folk flock here, too, traditionally from Midwestern cities like Cincinnati and St. Louis, occupying homes their families have held for generations.

Population increases by two thousand percent in summer, but the Pool still seems lazy, the way summer colonies are meant to be. Perhaps that's because not many other tourists come here.

"It's incredibly remote, no one can ever find it," commented an elderly summer resident, Mrs. Ross, to a reporter some years back. "Everything stays the same here, year in, year out. To give you a hint," she continued, "the most exciting thing people around here have to do is buy groceries and pick up their mail. It's always been like that—just, well, blah."

Blah, perhaps. But then there are cultures who spit on the beauty of their children, believing that a modicum of defilement will keep evil spirits at bay. Self-depreciation around Biddeford Pool is surely intended to shelter residents from the general populace. You'll find no advertisements about the area in tourist brochures, barely a mention of it at the Biddeford Chamber of Commerce. Though there is plenty of land open to the public at the Pool, the region definitely attempts to keep a low profile.

GETTING YOUR BEARINGS

Like an island, Biddeford Pool does seem removed from mainland concerns, which is odd, because Biddeford proper is a bustling community defined by its nineteenth-century mills, Franco-American heritage, and multitude of tourist attractions (like the Aquaboggan Park and Funtown U.S.A. a few miles north in Saco) inland on U.S. Route 1. The Pool is isolated from all that. There's no reason to go to the Pool except to be there. Yet, unlike an island, Biddeford Pool is accessible, a mere three-mile jaunt out State Route 208 from State Route 9 (eight miles in all from the center of Biddeford), not far beyond the campus of the University of New England, where the state's only medical school is located. Just so you know, State 9 looks like it moves south to north, but it's actually traveling west to east. That's Maine geography.

If approached from the west (south), the Pool appears to be an extension of Fortunes Rocks Beach just east of the Kennebunks.

In spite of its low profile, or perhaps because Biddeford Pool can't escape being part of Biddeford, the Pool has never quite succeeded in keeping out the people, just in limiting them. There's a sense that something has been preserved here, that even the visitor can partake of the summer colony at any time of year. And it's the mixture—the smells of the tiny fishing village that first attracted the summer colony, the tumble of homes large and small, the huge "pool" swarming with birds, and the broad, spacious white sand beaches near an equally spacious private golf course sporting its own church—that makes Biddeford Pool so entrancing.

Drive down the neck, where homes both modern and classic pile on a hill over crashing waves. Bear left past the post office to find an enclave of commercial establishments—the general store, a couple of gift shops, a take-out place offering lobster and clam rolls, and the area's only bed-and-breakfast inn. Keep going toward the gut (the narrow entrance to the pool that flows swiftly with the tides). You'll find the fishing village at the entrance to the Pool, the Biddeford Pool Yacht Club, and a dredged harbor that makes the Pool one of the best shelters in the region. The salt of the sea resides here. Lobster boats idle beside the pier. Lobster traps pile beside homes sheathed in shingles weathered to gray. In the harbor, there's a small island with a monument on it, an early navigational mark. I remember asking a fisherman the name of the island. "Monument Island," he replied. Of course. But its name really is Stage Island—named for the stages or racks on which early fishermen dried their fish before salting it and shipping the catch off to England.

The area across the gut is the Hills Beach area. This long, narrow peninsula packed with Victorian homes and beaches is equally full of history, should you wish to explore it.

In the distance stands Wood Island, where the Wood Island Light beckons both ships and herons. But ships avoid it, for the most part. Many are the tales of ships wrecked against the ocean side of the rocks, sometimes three at a time, smashed in the breakers. Herons, however, flock here, building nests in the spring.

When Samuel Champlain explored the region in 1603, he named the island the Isle of Bacchus because of the abundance of grapevines. Today, Wood Island is owned by the Maine Audubon Society and has neither grapevines nor many trees. Except for late spring, when the heron rookeries need their privacy, visitors are allowed on the island, but Maine Audubon prefers that you ask permission first.

Between Stage and Wood Islands is the island now known as Negro Island, earlier called Tappan, named after a man who ran a general store right there on the island, serving the fishing fleet that once swarmed through Saco Bay. Later it was called Nigger Island, one of some seven places in Maine given that label. (In the early 1970s, the state legislature changed the name to Negro Island.) But the reason for the name remains unclear. It could be that an African American family lived on the island, or simply that the island had a crop of Blue Spruce growing on it, which is so dark it has a black appearance.

BIRDING BIDDEFORD

From the fishing village, turn down Orcutt Boulevard, past the golf course to the East Point Sanctuary, a lovely ribbon of rosebush and raspberry, fierce rocks and cobble beach bathed in the precious, moist quiet of coastal Maine. This thirty-acre sanctuary, also cared for by Maine Audubon, is another of the area's bird havens. According to *A Birder's*

Wood Island Light

Guide to the Coast of Maine by Elizabeth Cary Pierson, Jan Erik Pierson, and Peter D. Vickery (which devotes a full chapter to Biddeford Pool), it is the geography, that the land extends into open ocean, that makes the Pool "a trap for migrant land birds and storm-tossed vagrants, and . . . a fine vantage point from which to scan for seabirds." Adds Bob Savage at Maine Audubon, "It's on the coastal flyway and it's undeveloped." While there are other points of land in Maine that extend to open ocean, much of the coast is either wooded or developed. The shrub and grass habitat of the sanctuary at Biddeford Pool offers an open invitation to many traveling species.

To see birds, come during spring and fall migration, and any other time as well. According to *A Birder's Guide*, "just about anything can turn up at any time of year and often does."

The guide mentions warblers, including orange-crowned warblers in the fall, as well as peregrine falcons and merlins. Look for (but don't disturb) plovers and sandpipers roosting on the rocks at high tide, and look on the adjacent golf course for lesser golden plovers, Baird's and buff-breasted sandpipers, and in winter for snowy or short-eared owls, rough-legged hawks, and northern shrikes. In winter, you might also see loons, grebes, and even harlequin ducks off the coast and purple sandpipers on the rocks.

The entrance to the sanctuary stands about twenty yards back, marked by a chain-link fence and a small sign. It's open to visitors sunrise to sunset, but because of the narrowness of the roads in the Pool, there is very limited parking. If you're so equipped, bicycle around the Pool, but leave your bike at the sanctuary gate. There's no picnicking, pets, or bikes allowed inside. Again, be careful of roosting birds.

At East Point, Orcutt Boulevard becomes Ocean Avenue. If you round the corner beyond the sanctuary, you'll find the old Coast Guard station, begun in 1874 (and staffed by men from the down east town of Jonesport), when it was known as a life-saving station. It still stands white and comforting, its large doors open to the water. (The Jonesport guardsmen stayed on in retirement and their descendants came to be known as the Jonesport aristocracy.) The road continues to South Point, with the ocean on one side and homes on the another. If you're into birding, check the tides and return to Fletcher Neck, inside the wide pool of Biddeford Pool, when the tide is either rising or falling, though not when it's high or low. According to *A Birder's Guide,* "feeding is generally most fervid on the falling tide, since the high tide has replenished the food supply and the birds have not fed for several hours." After asking permission at Hattie's Deli, you can walk a trail through the grass to the pool to find a wide range of shorebirds, including semipalmated and black-bellied plovers, killdeer, greater and lesser yellowlegs, spotted, least, and semipalmated sandpipers, ruddy turnstones, short-billed dowitchers and dunlins in the fall.

In spring and summer you might also see great blue herons, green herons, snowy egrets, black-crowned night herons, and glossy ibis. And in winter, you may find horned larks, snow buntings, and Lapland longspurs.

LOBSTER CLAIMS

After Champlain, sailing for France, visited the region in 1603, the English arrived. In 1616, Fernando Gorges, who once held title to most of southern Maine, sent his deputy, Richard Vines, to explore the region and determine whether it would be possible to winter over on the coast of Maine. Vines not only survived his winter on the mouth of the Saco River, he liked it so well that he named it Winter Harbor and returned in 1630 to establish a colony. But there was trouble with those who lived here already. The Native Americans were not pleased with the settlement, and skirmishes continued. So did the settling. By the 1670s, when early naturalist John Josselyn visited, he described the Pool as "one scattering town of large extent, well-stored with cattle, arable land and marshes and a saw mill."

The Pool soon became a fishing center, among the most important on the coast. In the early part of this century, around the fall harvest, a gill-netter could easily snag thousands of barrels of herring. As many as two hundred fishing boats, hailing from Boston to Eastport, fished inside the pool for herring, often leaving directly from the Pool for deepwater fishing grounds with the herring as bait. (The Biddeford Pool Yacht Club has some spectacular sepia prints of the fleet. Ask to see them.)

For centuries, swordfish, sturgeon, sea bass, bluefish, and lobster abounded here. In fact, a 1935 article in what is now the *Maine Sunday Telegram* claims that Biddeford Pool was the origin of the lobster industry in Maine. As the story goes, back in 1870, Frank Verrill noticed a lobster thrown up on the shore, took it home, and asked his wife to cook it for him. Five hours later (so the article says), Mrs. Verrill entered with a lobster on a platter. After puzzling over the shell, Verrill managed to get it off, taste the meat, and *voilà*, at five cents a beast an industry was born. The story, told by Verrill's nephew, Waldo Stillson Verrill, is a charming one. However, lobster was a known bait used by the Native Americans and early settlers. Yes, it was food, but only when the bait didn't take and fish wasn't forthcoming. So much for oral history. According to John Oddy, who runs The Lodge, the area's only bed-and-breakfast, local indentured servants made sure they had written into their contracts the stipulation that they not be served lobster more than five days a week. Whether for servants or rusticators lobstering had become a part of the fishing industry of Maine early in its history as a state. But it wasn't always lucrative. By 1840, lobsters—three-pounders— were going at two cents apiece in May and June.

RUSTICATORS

In the 1870s, only thirteen families lived in the Pool, but summer visitors were beginning to arrive, among them the family of Joseph W. Smith, whose celebration of the area, *Gleanings from the Sea*, can still be found at local shops. "There is no resort on the whole Atlantic coast that Biddeford Pool is second to as a summer watering place," Smith writes.

The Pool really got going as a summer colony around 1879, when New York developer Fred T. Brown laid out the golf course and built several cottages and inns. The most visible of the old inns is now the Marie Joseph Spiritual Center, a nondenominational spiritual retreat for people who, say the current owners, the Sisters of the Presentation, "want to experience sacred space and time." With its landscaped gardens and small pond, the sanctuary is a haven inside a haven.

As the hundred-room Ocean House during the late nineteenth century, it was quite a different sort of place, ringing with the laughter of children and the quiet conversations of proper English visitors from the predominantly French Canadian cities of Montreal and Quebec. The women and children came for the summer; their husbands joined them in August. "We went to the beach, went swimming, played tennis, went on the rocks, played croquet in the afternoon, had dinner at five with our nursemaids in the children's dining room and played games after dinner until seven when we were in bed," recalls Mrs. Mary Evans Clopper, whose parents ran the hotel until 1948 when they sold it to the Sisters of the Presentation.

Mrs. Clopper still lives in the Pool. Until late 1997, when her dog, Sadie, passed away, she and Sadie walked three and a half miles a day. Clopper's daughter, Eve McPheeters, also lives in town, in the house she grew up in, one of the few of her generation who remain in Biddeford Pool. "Careers and taxes took them away," says McPheeters.

By the early part of this century, some thirty to forty families from the Midwest were summering in Biddeford Pool, spending their days boating, bathing, and deep-sea fishing. Women in long skirts cast their lines from perches on the rocks. At night, all frequented one of many social gatherings in the Pool.

Such residents were augmented by guests at the two inns that were then part of town. But there seems to have been trouble for some in getting to the Pool. Artist James Montgomery Flagg, creator of the World War I recruiting poster "Uncle Sam Wants You," dubbed the winding road to the Pool "the valley of stones." And President William Howard Taft, who visited his sister here in 1910, stepped off the boat only to get his feet soaked—the float sunk under the weight of Taft's three hundred pounds.

THE PEOPLE AND THE BEACH

As much as summer residents may wish for exclusivity in Biddeford Pool, they have not quite achieved it. It's not like other Maine summer colonies, such as Ocean Avenue in nearby Kennebunkport, where George Bush has his summer home; or Grindstone Neck, a summer colony of Winter Harbor near Gouldsboro (depicted from the native Maine perspective in Sanford Phippen's novel *Kitchen Boy*).

In 1972, the feisty Biddeford administration of Mayor Gilbert Boucher decided it wasn't right for Biddeford to have a wide coastal expanse and no way for the citizens of town to enjoy it. Invoking eminent domain, the town took seven acres of beach from the privately owned Pool Beach Association for public use, catapulting the region to national prominence.

As the *Portland Press Herald* reported, "This marked the climax of the long, quiet battle, but it was by no means the end of it.

"While city officials were gloating over the national recognition they had attracted by taking the land, the wealthy summer residents were retaliating with a barrage of legal attacks, challenging everything from the constitutionality of the taking to the amount of damages ($250,000) awarded by the city."

In 1977, state court ruled that the taking of the land was constitutional, but raised the amount of damages, so that in the end, Biddeford paid over half a million for the seven-acre beach. Biddeford residents know it's worth it—the town has a vast expanse of glorious sand beach to visit, with a bit of surf and plenty of room for beach volleyball, Frisbee, and extensive castle and canal systems. Though much smaller, the beach is comparable to Old Orchard Beach to the north, and not at all overrun.

Parking, however, is still a problem. You can buy a seasonal parking permit for about fifty dollars, you can try to park near East Point, or you can simply pay by the day at Hattie's Restaurant, across the street from the public beach.

Perhaps because there's a fee for parking, the Pool's insular qualities do remain. Bicyclers come by, and visitors willing to pay to park, but this is no tourist mecca. There are a few signs directing people to the handful of stores—general store, gift shops, snack bar, bed-and-breakfast and the Biddeford Pool Yacht Club, but little indication of the beach. Don't worry, if you do get lost, all you need to do is swing around and come back. All roads lead to the same place.

Come fall, the homes shutter down and the three thousand-odd summer population dwindles to a skeleton of one hundred fifty, max. The casual visitor can easily find parking and relish the ghost town atmosphere.

As Mrs. Ross indicated, there is not much to do in Biddeford Pool, which is just right with most everyone who visits. There is, however, Oddy's The Lodge, with its own dock and beach, open year-round.

Holiday Lights

If you visit at Christmastime, be sure to drive around at night so as to delight in Biddeford's holiday lights. On the Pool Road (State 208 and 9), you'll find a yard with enough young trees to be a tree farm, and spiraling white lights strung around each one, turning the yard into a fairy wonderland.

More spectacular, however, is a trio of homes off State 9. As you leave Biddeford and start climbing the hill, look for a skating rink on your right. Two streets up from that is a small driveway of a road. Turn right onto it to find a group of homes whose lights will make you laugh out loud for the sheer exuberance of the display.

Again, every tree in every yard is ringed with lights. But there's more: Candy canes light up one driveway, along another the lights move in sequence. Lights frame each house, and each window of each house. Across the top of one is written NOEL, in lights, of course. A tent of lights cascading from a pole topped by a star provides a glowing shelter for a crèche. At another house, lights illuminate a huge Santa with all his reindeer.

A woman explained to me that many in Biddeford do what they can to light up these darkest of nights. She herself strings 5,500 lights outside her house. For a month, her electric meter speeds around, the bill ups by fifty dollars, but "it's just once a year," she says, "and it's fun."

Places to See, Eat, and Stay

Bufflehead's Restaurant, Hill's Beach: (207) 284-6000.

Days Lobster Pound, Biddeford Pool: (207) 282-0803.

F. O. Goldthwaite Store and Snack Bar, Biddeford Pool: (207) 284-8872.

Hattie's Restaurant, Biddeford Pool: (207) 282-3435.

P. M. Inness Lobster Co., Biddeford Pool: (207) 284-5000.

The Lodge, Biddeford Pool: (207) 284-7148.

Maine Audubon Society, Portland: (207) 781-2330.

Marie Joseph Spiritual Center, Biddeford Pool: (207) 284-5671 or (207) 283-0367.

McArthur Library, Biddeford: (207) 284-4181.

University of New England, Hills Beach: (207) 283-0171.

2

NEWFIELD: A MANUFACTURING HAMLET GROWN SMALL

Barbara O'Brien likes to invite people she meets on her forays to fairs and craft sales to visit the historic village of old Newfield. O'Brien is a potter who sells her own production ware out of her home in Newfield, a quiet hamlet in western Maine.

"If I had a nickel for all the people who stood in my shop door saying, 'This is what I want when I retire . . .'" laughs O'Brien, a bit ruefully. She's covered with clay from fingernails to boots at the end of a long day at her work, Barnswallow Pottery. You can hear in that laugh her sense of victory in living a life this rural and independent, but such an achievement carries very little of the ease one expects with retirement. O'Brien settled in Newfield around 1970. Her house, built one hundred years earlier, was once a stop-

ping place for travelers. Though it is no longer an
inn, and certainly no longer run-down, the
home continues to attract people to see O'Brien's
pottery, her yard full of cement garden ornaments,
and her attic of old books.

And yet, O'Brien fondly calls Newfield "Nowhere-
field." Practically at the border with New Hampshire, Newfield is a town defined by edges: the
northern edge of York County, the southern edge
of Maine's lake district, and the western edge of
the state. Although there are major through routes from New
Hampshire into Maine, and from southern Maine north-
ward, Newfield is on none of them, unless you try to call
State Route 11, passing right through town, a major route. It
isn't.

The genuineness of Newfield's remoteness is the reason it
is so frequently marked as the place people dream of when
they find themselves longing for life in the quiet of a small,
rural town. Many of the homes are old, the streets are over-
hung with trees, and the pace is very, very slow—much
slower, in fact, than the bustling era of small-town industry
captured in the historical museum that is at Newfield's heart.
Willowbrook is a village of a museum, begun in 1970 by Don
King, who came to Newfield in search of his own rural
dream.

Down the road from the museum, history segues into pre-
history at a pine barren filled with stunted, gnarled trees. It's
the kind of landscape you expect to find on the coast, where
sand, salt, and wind keep trees small, but this inland barren
grew in the wake of sand deposited by a retreating glacier
twelve thousand years ago. Recently saved from development
by Maine's Nature Conservancy, the barrens are a fascinating place for an afternoon walk. Nearby is the Little Ossipee
River, which rages with the spring tide, luring canoeists, only
to sedately amble through rocks come summer.

For these and other reasons, Newfield is about as perfect a small town as you can find, and yet it's within a half-hour drive of southern Maine's larger towns, including Gorham, where the University of Southern Maine is located. Perhaps that is why Newfield surprised itself recently with the news that its small expansion from retirement community had made it the fastest-growing town in York County.

HISTORY

Newfield has never rushed into growth. It was first traded in a package along with four other towns to a European, Francis Small, in 1668 by a sagamore known as Captain Sunday. According to the deed, signed by a mark of a turtle, Captain Sunday received in return for the land twenty miles square, "two large Indian blankets, two gallons of rum, two pounds of powder, four pounds of musket balls, and twenty strings of beads."

It wasn't until over a century later that some settlers from the coast came in to clear fields. Most then left for the winter, returning in spring to their new fields—hence the name Newfield. As with many towns in Maine, however, it wasn't until the Revolutionary War ended that Newfield developed a substantial population, fueled by returning soldiers claiming their promised land.

As settlers came, they took advantage of the many rivers and lakes of the region, building the small manufactories of the nineteenth century. By 1870, the population of Newfield had surpassed fifteen hundred, and local industry was thriving. There were grist mills, woolen mills, lumber mills, planing and stave mills in town, as well as a carding machine, a paper and board factory, an iron foundry from iron mined in the area, and several portable sawmills. Of all these, the carriage industry became most famous. Though Newfield is a remote town on the edge of the state, in the 1870s there were as many as five establishments building carriages and sleighs of all kinds in Newfield, while other industries supplied the carriage makers. This was the time when carriages were just becoming affordable to the farmer, who had previously used the farm's horse and wagon for forays into town.

According to Mary E. Doyle, who has compiled her history, nature, and profile columns for *The Sanford News* into a limited-edition book, *Newfield: Notes from Shady Nook*, tows of up to seven carriages in summer and possibly as many sleighs in winter "would be hitched together and hauled by a double-horse team to the railroad at Burleyville, New Hampshire," en route to Boston. Some three hundred carriages and wagons and four hundred sleighs were built in town each year, the sleighs being used in Newfield, as elsewhere in Maine, on snowy roads pressed with heavy wooden rollers pulled by a team of horses. (In a replica carriage barn built for the purpose, the range and kind of carriages and sleighs can be seen at Willowbrook, which has over sixty on display.)

But the industry was somewhat short-lived. Beginning around 1880, the double effect of southern New England's industrialization and the nation's westward expansion took its toll on small farming villages like Newfield. Population dropped by a third, to less than one thousand. By the turn of the century, even the carriage manufactories couldn't maintain themselves in the face of assembly lines, like those in Amesbury, Massachusetts. According to Doyle, a carriage similar to the one produced by hand in Newfield for between $45 and $100 could be found at prices beginning at $31.85 from the Amesbury assembly line.

It wasn't long, of course, before cars took over from carriages and isolation lessened for those who remained in Newfield. Come June and early July, farmers would drive as far as Old Orchard Beach and Biddeford to sell strawberries.

Then Newfield suffered another blow, this about half a century after the effects of industrialization. In October 1947, on a very windy day after a very hot and dry summer, a fire arose from a dropped cigarette on the outskirts of Newfield. With the wind blowing as hard as fifty miles an hour, fireballs hurled through the woods, sounding like an approaching freight train. Whole blazing treetops were tossed by the wind for hundreds of yards, igniting further flames. Many of the homes in town burned, as did much of the forest, with fire spreading to Shapleigh, south Waterboro, and Alfred. That same month, there was also a fire on Mount Desert Island, decimating the fine summer homes (known as cottages) built by the nation's rich and famous and altering the nature of Bar Harbor forever.

In Newfield, a sawdust pile smoldered for two years. A few homes were spared, others rebuilt, among them the homes where Willowbrook was founded and the home to which O'Brien eventually moved. The local library was also spared, thanks to the continued efforts of three young World War II veterans who ripped off burning clapboards to save the structure. (The library has since moved into the old elementary school building.) But since many of the forty homes and dozen public buildings were not rebuilt, Newfield looks smaller today than it would have in 1947.

MOULTON MILL

Surviving this catastrophe was the Moulton Mill, now over two hundred years old. The mill is located in West Newfield on State 11 at the point where the road makes a sharp turn.

When it was one hundred years old, in 1879, the mill was bought by Charles Moulton. The Moulton family ran the old mill until fairly recently, when they built a new mill up State 11 toward Limerick.

Moulton Lumber, now run by Charles Moulton's grandson, Allen Moulton, with help from Allen's son, Jim, keeps a small, museumlike room displaying old hand tools, a lathe, and some photos. Visitors are welcome.

The old mill was still a viable operation in 1976, sawing boards up to twenty-one inches wide with a Civil War–era water turbine, when Steve Libby wrote his bicentennial history of the town, *Newfield, Maine: The First 200 Years*. He writes:

> While the mill's exterior has for centuries attracted students to its humble beauty, its interior houses even more remembrances of things past. The original crudely-fashioned wooden mill wheel which ran the up-and-down sawmill is sheltered here, its wooden teeth of oaken pegs securely fastened, its iron bolts all handmade.
>
> Mostly under water throughout the year, an interesting "filter" arrangement resembles nothing more than a huge wooden comb. Its teeth are wooden poles. The unit—designed by an unknown inventor well over a century ago, allows the water to pass through but keeps out floating lumber, chips and other matter which would surely damage . . . the ancient water turbine below.

Unwilling to let the mill deteriorate, Marian and Anthony Tedeschi, who live up State 11 in Limerick, have bought the large complex, intending to eventually restore it and turn it into a museum. As Marian Tedeschi says, the mill's "best identity is that it be itself. It is the poetry of the thing," she adds, speaking slowly, deliberately, her voice infused with love and some degree of amazement at what she and her husband have taken on. "It's just a beautiful, beautiful place, one of the most photographed and painted sights in the area. The town and the Moultons loved it very much."

Of course, one and two hundred years ago, every town had several sawmills; they were essential to the building of the state. But few such mills are left, especially those reaching back to the eighteenth century. "There will be even fewer in twenty years," warns Tedeschi. "It seemed to us a critical time for that mill."

Recognizing that it is unusual for one person to launch a museum, Tedeschi is quick to point out a model, just down the road. "Willowbrook started the same way," she says. "It was one man's passion, and his wife's. I think the world would be happier if everyone followed their passions, at least the good ones. I think Willowbrook is one of the best small museums in the nation."

WILLOWBROOK

Don and Pan King came to Newfield at a time when the town was in something of a slumber. People may have come there to retire, but not to raise children. With a population of less than five hundred, the schools had shrunk. It was an easy place to acquire land, which was what Don and Pan King did, using the fortune they made in Texas oil to buy much of the center of town of Newfield proper (though a large part of Newfield lies in the village of West Newfield, near Moulton Lumber).

Most historical museums present a picture of wear and tear. The scuff marks of age are part of the picture, an insistence that viewers recognize that items were used and a means of showing them how they were used.

Willowbrook has a different philosophy. At Willowbrook, the exhibits are as bright and shiny as if they were just delivered from the Sears Roebuck catalog, or the carriage maker down the road. The peddler wagon is a bright red, the milk wagon a creamy yellow, the wedding wagon gleams spotless white. You can be sure, in this town known for building carriages, that carriages have a prominent place at Willowbrook.

The gleam here conveys better than anywhere else a sense of nineteenth-century optimism, the frequent prosperity, and in the carriages, the memory of the westward expansion of a nation so eager for the new that New England towns found themselves decimated.

Walk through the William Durgin Homestead, part inn and part fine country home, or the more modest home of Dr. Isaac Trafton, with its "unmarried maiden's room" built for Dr. Trafton's niece. The rooms are neat as a pin, but also airy and bright. Enjoy the oddments of a century ago, old pumps, bicycles, a "roadable aeroplane," and the Newfield Plumbing Shop, displaying the fascinating artifacts most museums ignore: an old zinc bathtub, a copper hot water tank, an early "flush."

Do you hear the lilting of a century-old barrel organ? Follow your ears. It accompanies the village's prize possession, an 1894 Armitage-Herschell carousel—the most complete original carousel in the nation. The carousel cannot be ridden, but it can be watched. And like everything else in this rambling museum, it is delightfully preserved, with reds and yellows shining as they would have a century ago.

The late Don King had a bit of a fear of museums, thinking of them as dark, stuffy rooms. He hoped his historical village would not be seen as a museum, but as a form of entertainment. According to Georgia Perry, who directs the museum with King's widow, Pan (who is also an award-winning ballroom dancer), there is ample evidence for his concern. "The first year we were open, we didn't have time to restore, and the schoolkids just shrugged," says Perry. "The second year, when we had everything fixed up, the children wanted to touch everything."

King began this operation in 1968 as a labor of love, buying up buildings in the village of Newfield and adding nineteenth-century farm and trade implements. The village now includes two complete houses, a general store, several barns, the carousel, a meeting hall, some two dozen trade shops, and collections of musical instruments, toys, sewing machines, creamers, and farm implements—an antiquer's delight, but for looking only. The museum surrounds a picturesque old mill pond, with its mill house still standing.

Georgia Perry came to Willowbrook before the curtains had gone up in the museum; her job was to restore the upholstery. Today, Perry still spends winters restoring upholstery and most anything else that needs work. Her summers are spent running the village.

The center of operations here is a general store, where tickets are sold, information provided, and a wide assortment of penny candy offered. Up the road, Pan King runs a Christmas store. There's also a small lunch counter and picnic tables.

But the willows of Willowbrook have been lost. Crushed by the heavy ice that built up over days of freezing rain during the great ice storm of January 1998, most of the willows were downed along with the town's power lines. While lines can be restored, the willows could not be.

A Cautionary Tale

Not every Newfield dream works out. For a time, Kathy Werking and her former husband, Russell Kivatisky, tried out a dream they had of living a rural life. They came here on a visit from Louisville, Kentucky, during the foliage season of 1995. Said Werking, "We were looking for someplace out in the country and we stumbled onto Newfield. We heard there was a museum there. We went to the museum and saw there was a house for sale by the owner. The deal worked out; it was serendipitous."

The downside of living a rural life is often expressed in the amount of driving it requires. Just to get to a supermarket, people in Newfield must drive twenty-five miles. Then there's the question of earning a living. Moving to Newfield was not exactly a move up the career ladder for either Werking or Kivatisky. Both have Ph.D.s in communication. While Kivatisky taught communication at the University of Southern Maine, Werking spent her work week driving around southern Maine juggling three part-time teaching and administrative jobs.

In her spare time, she tried to launch an upscale gourmet food shop, The New England Pantry. For a time, the couple relished Newfield life. Even the isolation seemed to have benefits, said Werking. "There's a nice sense of community that is surely brought about by geographical circumstances. You have the sense of helping people out here, of loaning back and forth, sharing garden equipment and ladders, helping each other on construction equipment. There's a working barter system, which is refreshing."

As an example, she spoke of Denise Carpenter, who lives in the mill house on the mill pond that is near the center of Willowbrook, though not a part of the museum. "Denise isn't afraid of getting up on a ladder and doing roofs," said Werking. "Just last summer she went down and redid the roof of Barbara O'Brien, the potter, in exchange for pottery. We give each other our time and our various skills. Money doesn't exchange hands at all."

But the isolation proved too much for Werking and Kivatisky. By 1997, they had given it up; she left Newfield for her Kentucky horse country, he for Portland, Maine's largest city.

SUGARING OFF

Such defections are rare in Newfield, however. Most people who come stay for the duration, growing accustomed to the cycle of busy summers and hunkering-down winters.

Come early November, the stores in the center of town—Barnswallow Pottery, Christmas, Etc., and others—offer an open house. Come March, it's the maple syrup of Bruce Bryant that lures visitors, for Bryant's sons Mark and Michael run Hilltop Boilers, one of three area sugar houses.

Some say sleepy, out-of-the-way Newfield wakes up only at this time, on Maine Maple Sunday, the third Sunday in March, when over two thousand people from throughout southern Maine visit area sugar houses. Bryant has lived in Newfield about twenty years, moving to his farm from East Dixfield, an equally small town farther north. Bryant may not be native to Newfield, but he knows farming. "My family goes back fifteen generations of farmers," he says. The farm he grew up on is a seventh-generation farm. Today, though he augments the farm work with construction, he calls farming "a growing part of the operation. We cut and baled and delivered seventy-five hundred bales of hay last year," he says, much of it on land owned by others. "We also raise Scotch highland cattle and sell freezer beef, and we do custom tractor work. We have a pair of working ponies that we use for hayrides, sleigh rides, and take to a few parades." Behind the ponies, Bryant lugs what is known as a Democrat

Wagon, or a buckboard—the forerunner of the station wagon or pickup, with two seats up front and space behind to carry cargo.

Bryant likes the sense of neighborliness in Newfield, despite the changes in town. "Everyone knows everyone. Everyone lends a hand," he says.

Making maple syrup is not a losing proposition, but it's not terribly lucrative, either. Like much that happens in Newfield, tapping trees is a work of the heart. Young Ashley Gerry also taps maples in Newfield, at Sugar Hill, and Douglas and Debbie Morin tap trees on their land down State 11 just over the line in Limerick.

Says Debbie Morin, "If you ever meet any serious maple syrup producers, they're all of a kind. They're like hunters, the sap runs, and their hair stands on end. It's in their blood." She laughs a moment. "It's in my husband's blood. We just humor him." For the month of March, when the nights are cold but the days are warm enough to get the sap running, humoring him may mean staying up all night, with twenty-four-hour-straight boils while the sap is running.

Though Maine Maple Sunday (the third Sunday of March) is the traditional time to come by to see the sap boil, Morin, like Bryant, says that she can be visited almost any time in March. "Anytime we're boiling, anytime you see steam coming off, we're open," she says.

WATERBORO PINE BARRENS

Not five miles down Bridge Street from Willowbrook (Bridge Street being the road that bears right off State 11 barely a quarter mile east of Willowbrook), the Nature Conservancy has opened a trail through a rare northeast pine barren.

Gnarled trees are not unusual in Maine. At the coast and along high mountain ridges, stunted trees, with their toughened, knuckled limbs clawing out in all directions, are quite common. But to find such a forest on a low-lying inland plain is most unusual. And to be surrounded by it—by acres of knobby pitch pine trees, with bristling needles growing straight from the bark in places—turns a short walk through moss-covered woods into an odd, fairyland excursion.

The Nature Conservancy considers the Waterboro Barrens one of the largest and most important acquisitions of recent years, worth every dollar of the $1.3 million spent. And yet, as the conservancy's Bruce Kidman admits, "It's the kind of site that you might well walk through or drive by, and unless someone tells you why it's special, and why so few of such barrens are intact, why they're so rare, why they're important to protect, you might not understand it as something special."

Like blueberry barrens, pine barrens are anything but desolate or barren. In Waterboro, scrub oak grows knee deep above a forest floor of blueberries, moss, and sweet fern. Unusual species like the rattlesnake weed, also known as Poor Robin's plantain, which is rare in Maine, and the endangered fern-leafed false foxglove, grow alongside the trails. Above, the pitch pine sends out its craggy boughs.

Fluttering among them are an array of birds, including pine warblers, rufous-sided towhees, brown thrashers, eastern bluebirds, prairie warblers, whippoorwills, and woodcocks. And, at sunset, a flurry of moths come to feast on the pitch pine and scrub oak that are essential for larvae, turning sections of the barrens into a winged blizzard. Among the moths are at least eight rare species.

These barrens are caused by an unusual inland deposit of sand. When the last glacier left Maine twelve thousand years ago, it played tricks on the land. Retreating, the glacier carried sand and gravel miles inland before the ice melted, depositing the sand in drifts up to seventy and eighty feet deep. Over Pine Springs Lake, which borders the conservancy land, bare ridges look more like Cape Cod's sand dunes than Maine's tough granite.

That the sand is nutrient-poor means scruffy vegetation like shrub oak and pitch pine thrive. That the sand so easily drains water means that these once-common barrens have become rare. The good drainage generally makes such barrens an excellent ground for commercial development.

To preserve the habitat of the Waterboro Barrens, the conservancy has added only a few new trails to the area. Most of the trail system runs along old jeep roads. These are so sandy that you might disconcertingly find yourself looking for an ocean. The section closest to the parking lot is most satisfying for its forest walk and distant glimpses of Pine Spring Lake. If you take the longer hike, a four-mile round-trip to the northern part of the preserve, you will get to hillier terrain and a ridge looking over wetlands created by the Harvey Mill Stream to Maine's southern hills beyond.

If you visit the region in spring, you might wish to tie a canoe on your car, as a trip on the Little Ossipee River, beginning perhaps in North Shapleigh on State 11 and extending through Newfield, is considered by the Appalachian Mountain Club *New England Canoeing Guide* to be one of the best and most beautiful trips in southern Maine. It dries up early, however. Unless the season is wet, by late April it may be too low to run some parts. You can put in at Shapleigh Pond, on Mann Road, one and a half miles below North Shapleigh, and run to Newfield. The guide describes this section as "marshy and winding, with several small rapids and a few beaver dams." You might still be able to see the damage from the 1947 fire on the banks of the river, but you'll find that there are many sections where the river is quite wild, with no visible dwellings. Instead, if you're quiet, you might find moose or deer or scare up a ruffed grouse. Just as you get into Newfield, there will be some ledges and lively rapids. The quick water continues to Ossipee Mills, six miles beyond. Watch out especially for two rare turtles, the endangered eastern box turtle and the threatened spotted turtle. Both have been seen on the Little Ossipee in Newfield.

If you know where you're going, it's easy to find Newfield and the Waterboro Barrens Preserve. To get there from southern Maine, take State 4 through North Berwick to Sanford, turning left onto States 4A and 109 and continuing straight on that road, which becomes States 11 and 109. State 11 leads directly into Newfield. To get to the Waterboro Pine Barrens from Newfield, turn down Bridge Street, or the Newfield Road. After about four miles, turn left onto Sherburne Lake Road (if you go too far, you'll get to a crossroads at Ross Corner), then turn right and continue one mile to Buff Brook Road. Turn left. At the end of the road you will see a parking area on the left. Trails lead from there.

Places to See, Eat, and Stay

Barnswallow Pottery: (207) 793-8044.

Christmas, Etc: (207) 793-2784.

Hilltop Boilers: (207) 793-8432.

Jeremiah Mason House Bed & Breakfast, Limerick: (207) 793-4858.

Morin Maple Syrup: (207) 793-8420.

Moulton Lumber: (207) 793-2541.

Newfield Historical Society: (207) 839-3666.

Sugar Hill Maple Syrup: (207) 793-8513.

Waterboro Barrons Preserve: (207) 729-5181 or (207) 490-4012.

Willowbrook at Newfield: (207) 793-2784.

Woodside Cottage Antiques: (207) 793-4502.

3

WALDOBORO'S
UNSUNG SURVIVALS

Twice daily the Medomak River empties to a broad mudflat packed with clams, then fills again to coastal splendor. Above it lies Waldoboro, a classic, stalwart town.

Lying a few hundred yards off the U.S. Route 1 tourist queue, not far from the famed Moody's Diner, Waldoboro village abides within the serenity of the road not taken. As if the steady flow and ebb of the river were change enough, Waldoboro's brick buildings and elegant architecture continue to recall its twined heritage of eighteenth-century German immigrants and nineteenth-century shipbuilders, while Waldoboro's current enterprises reflect a 1950s small town.

Like other places in Maine, the village of Waldoboro was preserved precisely because it was ignored, because U.S. 1 pushed away from Main Street, cushioning the town from the crowding of other coastal towns like Boothbay, Wiscasset, and Camden. The downside, of course, is that some businesses founder without more input from off U.S. 1. Barbara Howlett, who used to run a bookstore/café in Waldoboro, summed up the best and the worst of it, saying, "People just won't make the turn off Route 1; they don't come into Waldoboro." Most residents of the area agree that the gas stations, supermarket, and space-age, arrowhead-shaped bank that form the vision of town from the highway have very little to do with Waldoboro, though Moody's, Maine's most famous diner, certainly does.

Moody's has been a fixture of U.S. 1 for seventy years—wherever U.S. 1 happened to be. When the highway went through town, Moody's was there. At the time, Moody's was but a small restaurant and lunch wagon built to service the fling of tourist cabins the Moody family had built along the road in 1927. When U.S. 1 got rerouted out of town in the early 1930s, Percy Moody followed, trailering his lunch stand out to the highway and building a connecting road to be sure his cabins would still stand on U.S. 1. As the traffic increased, the Moodys expanded. The most recent expansion, completed in 1994, brought radiant heating into the old-style diner and raised seating to 108. But the Moody family knew better than to fool with the restaurant's famous neon sign, its diner exterior, and its worn wooden booths. People flock to Moody's for the atmosphere and all that it implies: Saturday night beans, breakfast any time, late night road stops, and the five dozen blueberry, rhubarb, and banana cream pies baked daily. They may not know it, but they're usually also getting fresh, Maine-grown food, another, quieter hallmark of the diner.

"AN UNSUNG, UNKNOWN PLACE"

But Moody's is taken for granted among Mainers. The questions Mainers ask about Waldoboro have not to do with its diner but its five-and-dime.

Who would ever think the five-and-dime would become such a rare and precious thing, such a trove of nostalgia? Here are sold both children's socks and a needle and thread with which to darn them, a plain pot in which to boil a dinner and the spice to put inside. The Waldoboro 5 & 10, located on Main Street, is the storehouse of childhood memories, the epitome of 1950s domesticity, with aisles so close that neighbors literally bump into each other as they browse, never knowing what will be in the next bin. Perhaps you'll find an apple peeler, perhaps a china cat, perhaps a sweatshirt proclaiming: "Waldoboro, pop. 4,601, deer 582, moose 96, fishermen 27, clams 2,682,174.

Presiding over the red flocking, children's toys, and hardware is Emily Trask-Eaton, an outspoken spokeswoman of the town. Trask-Eaton has owned the 5 & 10 for over a decade and has weathered the opening of a Wal-Mart, only about a dozen miles east in Rockland. But Trask-Eaton put the store on the market in 1997. It will keep going, but not with her—at the age when many start wondering about retirement, she's going to medical school.

Waldoboro, she says, "is an unsung, kind of unknown place. People think of it as U.S. Route 1 and Moody's, but writers, musicians, artists—interesting people—live here, both local and from away."

Trask-Eaton suggests people visit Waldoboro for what she calls a 1950s-style vacation. Perhaps she's referring to the idea that one could take a quiet, well-rounded rest here, walking through nearby nature preserves, visiting galleries and historic sites, bowling in the local alley, and wandering through town, enjoying antique stores, gift shops, and a few Waldoboro specialties. These reveal an eclectic assortment of interests: The Purple Foot, wine maker's haven, caring for the needs of the home brewer of beer and wine; the Rosearie at Bayfields out on State Route 32, a greenhouse specializing in, as they say, "practical roses for hard places"; and Central

Asian Artifacts, a basement store run by a former school administrator filled with unusually fine rugs.

His name is Jeff Evangelos, and he took a trip to the Near East one year. Though he came home, he never returned to school. Now he makes yearly journeys along the ancient silk route, commissioning rugs that he ships from Maine across the nation. His business, like The Purple Foot, the Rosearie, a couple of computer-oriented businesses, and the well-known Maine Antiques Digest, have updated the small-town dream of the 1950s to the 1990s by managing cross-country businesses from rural outposts.

Other Waldoboro businesses remain very local. The town has one of the few remaining independent pharmacies in the state. Druggist Ted Wooster knows nearly everyone in town; he knew their parents, too. Clark's Drug stands down the block from The Pine Cone, a bakery/café and a favorite place to settle over hot cider on a damp day. (And then there's Borealis Breads, located in a brightly painted building out on U.S. Route 1. Its sourdough bread is widely sought.)

But not everything in Waldoboro has thrived. Down by the river stands the four-story button factory that once punched mother-of-pearl buttons out of seashells. The nineteenth-century factory closed down a few years ago (its last manager was Jim Eaton, husband to Emily Trask-Eaton of the five-and-dime). Today, while some citizens are trying to figure out what to do with the lovely, stately building, others scout around outside to find pink-edged shells scalloped into bracelets by the button machines.

A final survival from the early part of this century is the Waldo Theatre, a 1936 vintage movie theater with art deco touches, courtesy of New York lumber dealer Carroll T. Cooney and New York architect Benjamin Schlanger, who is rumored to have been one of the architects of Radio City Music Hall in New York City. In early brochures, the theater billed itself as "Maine's little Roxy." The theater was a popular spot when it first opened. The waiting line for the thirty-five-cent daily shows frequently went around the block. Inside were hearing aids for those who had trouble hearing (despite the theater's powerful acoustics) and a contact system for patrons who might need to respond to a call during the movie. The theater advertised ample free parking, never mentioning it was in the apple orchard out back.

Like many theaters across the state, the Waldo closed in the late 1950s. The sump pump was shut off. Water rose onto the base-ment stairs, turning the building into a "wired sauna" according to the theater's newsletter. But unlike most other theaters, this one did not die. Volunteers re-opened it briefly for live stage productions in the 1980s. A few years later, it was bought by pianist and producer Kitty Fassett, who helped fund needed renovations. In 1990, the Waldo Theatre reopened again. It continues to offer movies, concerts, and local live theater productions on a regular schedule.

HOME OF THE FIVE-MASTED SCHOONER

A 1950s vacation might also include a look at Waldoboro's nineteenth-century survivals, like the elegant Italianate library next to the Waldo Theatre. It was once a U.S. cus-toms house, and remains a reminder of the days when Wal-doboro was a thriving port. Harking back to that era stands the Hutchins House, at 77 Main Street, now a funeral home. This wooden building is built in what is known as Stick Style; it is lovely and important enough to be placed on the National Register of Historic Places.

The original owner of the home was the builder of the famous Palmer fleet of schooners. These ships followed upon the heels of Waldoboro's heyday of shipbuilding, just before the Civil War, when Waldoboro was the sixth largest port in the United States in tonnage of ships registered. Waldoboro did not quite regain her stature as a shipbuilding port after the Civil War, but the town did retain some fame. It was 1888 when the *Gov. Ames* left her ways. She was 245 feet long, weighed 1,778 tons, and had five masts on her decks, the first of the five-masted ships to be built on the Atlantic seaboard (two smaller ships, one on the Great Lakes and one in Oregon, had previously tried five masts).

At first, the ship seemed to herald nothing. The *Gov. Ames*, it is said, stalled on the ways; a terrible omen at a launching. It was a decade before another five-masted ship was built, that one in Bath. Then, between 1900 and 1904, six five-masted schooners were built by George Welt of Waldoboro (the former owner of the Hutchins House) for William F. Palmer of Boston.

To my abidingly unnautical eye, the five-masted schooner —and the six-masted ones built just a few miles north in Rockland—are purely playful, ships drawn with the exuberance of a child who clearly knows that more is better. But the five-masters were neither exuberant nor romantic. They were economical. The rigging of these ships, known as the great schooners, could be done by steam winches; the setting of their sails could be handled by but a few sailors—one for every two hundred or two hundred and fifty tons, as opposed to one per every one hundred tons on the earlier square-rigged ships.

Used for carrying coal around the coast, they were considered fully modern, with steam heat, telephone connections throughout the vessels, safety appliances, and sounding devices. The ordinary sailor had more comfort on these than captains did fifty years earlier.

But visit Waldoboro at low tide and the very idea of it ever being prominent as a shipbuilding town appears unbelievable. When the tidal Medomak River empties out, there's hardly an inch of water to be seen. There is, instead, a sizable mud flat, hence the age-old prominence of clam digging. Ship launchings frequently waited for the spring tide, when the flow increased from nine to eleven feet.

The shipbuilding portion of Waldoboro's past is mostly hidden now, but as you walk around the banks of the Medomak you might see some small streams flowing in. Look there to see if there's a stubby framework of wooden beams rising through the mud. Here a ship would have been built.

A more visible memory of the shipping life is the town's architecture. Except for the plain facade of a new elderly housing complex downtown, much of the town's early architecture remains, a prominence of pre–Civil War excellence. Trask-Eaton offers her own house as an example. Built in the 1850s by a former sea captain, "it has eight marble fireplaces, each with a different kind of marble," she says. The marble, she adds, came to Waldoboro as ballast via ports in Italy.

Trask-Eaton is fascinated by the secrets told by these old homes. "In the house next door to me," she says, "there's a funny little bricked-up place in the basement which they found when they dug it up for a sewer project. Opening up the bricked-in walls, the workers discovered a tunnel leading underneath the street to another home." This tunnel could have been used to run bootleg liquor, since the selling of spirits, except for medicine or industrial purposes, was outlawed as early as 1846; it could have been a passageway for the underground railroad; it could also have conducted lovers on secret trysts between their homes.

There are more public hideaways in town—galleries, antique stores, the Waldoborough Historical Society Museum, with its one-room red schoolhouse from 1857, town pond (where animals were kept), and barn filled with old toys, tools, and period costumes. There are also several bed-and-breakfasts, among them Le Va-Tout, where the Eliza Sweet Gallery is located. It is gathering renown for its sculpture gardens that mingle sculpture and garden, designed by former owner Don Slagel. Sometimes the sculptures are literally hidden among the foliage, turning garden into sculpture.

GERMANS IN THE WILDERNESS

Though Le Va-Tout flaunts a French name, Waldoboro is a German town. By 1739, the settlement of Maine, particularly the northern and eastern portions, was not going as fast as its proprietors wished. Maine's harsh winters, bug-ridden summers, and deadly raids by the French and Native Americans at any time of year took some of the charm off the colonial adventure. To gain profit from their land, the proprietors had some convincing to do.

General Samuel Waldo did just that, assuring a group of Germans from around Bremen of the riches awaiting them in the New World. To these hapless citizens, Waldo painted a vivid picture of a thriving city in the wilderness of his Waldoborough (as it was then written). Adding injury to insult, the boatload of immigrants arrived in fall, when even the Abenaki Wawenock tribe had abandoned the fish-laden coast for inland forests. For the privilege of struggling over their hundred-acre plots, the Germans had paid Waldo five shillings and a rental of one peppercorn a year. Over a century later, the bitterness still lingered. Read the inscription on a marker at the Old German Cemetery, near the peach-colored 1772 Old German Church (painted by Andrew Wyeth in his *Maidenhair*, which is at the Farnsworth Museum in Rockland):

This town was settled in 1718 [sic], by Germans who emigrated to this place with the promise and expectation of finding a populous city, instead of which they found nothing but a wilderness; for the first few years they suffered to a great extent by Indian wars and starvation. By perseverance and self denial, they succeeded in clearing lands and erecting mills. At this time a large proportion of the inhabitants are descendants of the first settlers. This monument was erected A.D. 1855 by the subscriptions of citizens of this town.

The Germans not only survived, they prospered and remained intact. John Miller, a former press secretary to Governor Angus King, Maine's independent leader, was born and raised in Waldoboro. His grandfather gave the town land for a school, Miller Grade School, leaving the young Miller rather abashed, he says. The community was so tight that when Miller's father had sought to marry his mother they encountered grave displeasure. His mother was not German. In over two hundred years of Miller presence in Waldoboro, this was the first union outside the clan.

This German heritage accounts for one final Waldoboro survival, Morse's Sauerkraut, located up State Route 220 near the Washington town line. Morse's makes fresh sauerkraut and ships it in its brine to sustain Saturday night bean suppers from Florida to Hawaii, but especially in Michigan, Minnesota, and Wisconsin.

Before the automobile age, everyone made their own sauerkraut, just as they pressed their own cider and tapped their own maples and baked their own bread. Indeed, compared to sugaring off, sauerkraut making was easy. It was simply a matter of chopping up the cabbage and leaving it to cure in a brine of sugar, salt, and water.

Virgil Morse, Sr., did just that. He made such a tasty blend that in 1910, the local general store owner asked him to bring one of his barrels around to the store. He did, rather reluctantly, as it seemed an odd thing to do. But Morse's sauerkraut was a hit. Soon people were traveling to Waldoboro just for the kraut, and Morse was going into business for himself.

The business stayed within the Morse family until 1994, when it almost folded. An out-of-town buyer saved it and installed Greg Learned as manager and day-to-day operations man. Many rejoiced. "Cold weather without our sauerkraut is just too hard," said one elderly gentleman. He could be speaking for a crowd. The lure of the fresh, crunchy kraut reaches far and wide in Maine.

As in years back, Saturdays are the busiest, with locals flocking to the bunkerlike production building, container in hand, to procure the kraut essential to round out a meal of Saturday night sausage (preferably kielbasa) and beans. "I can remember coming here as a child, driving up from Durham [near Freeport], over dirt roads, just for the kraut," Learned says.

Though plastic barrels are now used instead of the old wooden barrels, and the new shredding machine employs blades so finely hewed they cost a thousand dollars a blade, production is basically the same as it ever was. Green cabbage is carted from a storage shed to the factory floor in an old green wooden handcart, stuffed into the shredder, scooped into the barrels, and then weighed down by a lid covered with heavy stones.

The appearance is downright arcane, if not frightening. The brine foams above the stones, turning green when it contacts the air, as if some energetic child had filled the large warehouse with numerous science projects and then forgotten about them. The foaming green of the barrels looks like a process gone terribly wrong; it most definitely does not look like real food production. But after two weeks, beneath the stones and a layer of rather moldy brine lies a flavorful sauerkraut—a world of difference from the soggy, smoky kraut to which most of us are accustomed.

WALDOBORO WORKERS

Watching the customers go to Morse's, walking the streets of town, you may think Waldoboro is a well-scrubbed retirement community. But retired local history teacher and former state legislator Bill Blodgett insists it is really a blue-collar commuter town. Some Waldoboro residents work at the nearby Osram Sylvania plant, makers of filament coils for lightbulbs. Others commute to Bath Iron Works, about twenty-five miles down U.S. Route 1, or to Rockland and Augusta. There are also some small businesses nearby, such as Common Sense Designs, a clothing manufacturer down the road in Nobleboro; Maine Antiques Digest, which has grown to be a feisty foundation of the antique business; The Science Source, a maker of science kits for schools; and a new arrival, the twenty-four-hour New England 800, a telephone answering and phone order service located in a former Odd Fellows Hall.

Others get by the Maine way, digging clams now that a cleanup has allowed the beds to be reopened, and pursuing various other seasonal labors, including lobstering, fishing, dairy and egg farming. Nathan Nichols is one of the seasonal laborers. His home is on State 32, not far from the much-visited German Cemetery, where the grumbling monument to the German arrival still stands. The Germans carved their complaint. Nichols welds his.

Nichols's lawn is decorated with ingenious planes created from junk parts—bicycle wheels and lawn mower handles—

with propellers that rotate and frames that swing in the wind. He is a dump picker, whom recent laws against removing items from the dump has transformed into what he calls a "dump thief." He scavenges dumps at night, returning with junked lawn mowers, which he easily fixes for sale. He also finds other treasures, most of which he simply stored on his lawn, until he happened to read the local newspaper one day.

"They put my name in the papers for operating a junk yard without a license," he explains. "They didn't even tell me. It is a tactic used by the town to embarrass people."

Nichols retaliated. First he threatened to weld his yard-side collection into a wall of junk art. Then he began working. "I'm not in it for the money, I'm just kind of decorating the yard," he says. He also fields numerous questions from people who stop to gawk. That his artwork encourages cars to stop at a particularly dangerous curve on State 32 doesn't bother Nichols any. "I like to get at people," he says.

Places to See, Eat, and Stay

Backdoor Bookstore: (207) 832-4613.

Borealis Breads: (207) 832-0655.

Broad Bay Inn & Gallery: (207) 832-6668.

Central Asian Artifacts: (207) 832-4003.

Clark's Drug Store: (207) 832-5511.

DePatsy's Bowling Lanes: (207) 832-5558.

Downeast School of Massage: (207) 832-5531.

Paul Fuller Antiques, (207) 832-5550.

Le Va-Tout Bed and Breakfast and Eliza Sweet Gallery: (207) 832-4969.

Maine Antique Digest, Inc: (207) 832-7534.

Moody's Diner: (207) 832-7785.

Moody's Motel: (207) 832-5362.

Moravian Settlement Site: Friendship Road.

Morse's Sauerkraut: (207) 832-5569.

Old German Meeting House: (207) 832-5100.

Pine Cone Cafe: (207) 832-6337.

Purple Foot Down East, Inc: (207) 832-6286.

Roaring Lion Inn: (207) 832-4038.

Rosearie at Bayfields: Practical Roses for Hard Places: (207) 832-5330 or (800) 933-4508 (messages only).

Tide's End Riding Stables: (207) 832-4431.

Guy Van Dyne Nature Trail: State Route 220 South.

Waldo Theatre: (207) 832-6060.

Waldoboro 5 & 10 Cent Store: (207) 832-4624.

Waldoboro Public Library: (207) 832-4484.

Waldoboro Town Forest: Junction of Old U.S. 1 and U.S. 1 South.

Waldoborough Historical Society Museum: State Route 220.

4

THAT HOUSE IN CUSHING

(RIVER ROAD, SOUTH OF THOMASTON)

In Cushing, the wind sweeps up the St. George River and over Hathorn Point, stirring faint odors of lilac and lime on its way to the Olson House. Inside the house, a shaft of light forms an angular shape over the floor's wide pine boards. As if stirred by the wind, dust dances in the rays that enter the low windowpanes. Here, within the Olson House's bare walls, the air seems to take form, molding our senses to its scent.

No matter that this weathered farmhouse, once the home of the woman made famous in Andrew Wyeth's *Christina's World*, is officially a museum. No matter that it has been shorn of furniture, and that other visitors shuffle behind you, peering at pictures, poking into closets. The silence lingers. This home is a shrine.

The faithful flock here, stalking the deep snowdrifts in winter, when the building is closed for the season, fogging the windows with their curious breath. They come in summer, when the museum is again open. They trudge downhill to the cemetery where Christina Olson lies buried. The more fervent fall to the ground to be photographed in a position they know by heart, the sprawling crawl in which Christina was painted, edging up the hill from her mother's grave to the house of her childhood. Perhaps they then feel the fierce determination that led the crippled woman to walk on her ankles when her feet had curled so she could no longer tread on her soles, to crawl when she could no longer use her ankles, and to huff her chair through the house when she could no longer crawl. To the end she refused a wheelchair.

Christina Olson most likely suffered from Still's disease, a progressive form of arthritis. As a child, she spent happy years running over the hills even though her mother had to swathe her knees with pads because she fell so much. In early photos of Christina, we find bright, eager eyes that seem to see everything, and a clever, witty face. At age eighteen, this bold and curious woman traveled to Boston to seek a doctor's advice. It was then she found out that there would be no cure. He told her to go home and lead a quiet country life.

Christina returned to the farm she was raised on; that trip to Boston remained her longest voyage. Though over the years her frame grew heavier, her arms never did. The reach of her arm used to be visible to the visitor—above that, the walls never could get clean. After years of heating and cooking with a wood stove, the higher portion of the walls had grown nearly black.

Christina and her brother Alvaro stuck it out their way, holding the farm long after they could work it, refusing assistance, forcing friends like the Wyeths to scramble for ruses just to help them out. Then, on Christmas Eve of 1967, Alvaro died. Thirty-four days later, Christina followed.

The wood stove is still in the home, but most other household goods are gone, having been sold at auction shortly after the owners' deaths. Today, the very absence of personal items illuminates the house, leaving the rooms like empty canvases transformed by coastal Maine's shifting sun. Against the

The Olson House

wood and light, visitors can project their private notions of
the stoic farmer and rural survivor who have become part of
our national heritage.

Despite the pain and poverty that marked the life
Christina shared with her brother, want is not what lingers
here. The remaining odors, like the dust, are of age. Like
any shrine, the heartache that built it has been mediated by
time, transformed into myth.

The bard of this myth is painter Andrew Wyeth, who captured so well the quiet heroics of Christina and her
fisherman-farmer brother. In Wyeth's paintings of Christina
and the Olson house, we find an image of the way we Americans wish we were, caught at the very cusp of our leaving it.
The Olsons represent the independence of the rural ideal, be
it as lobsterman, lumberman, cowboy, or farmer. Christina's
world preceded welfare, agricultural subsidies, handicapped

accessibility. Without glorifying those harsher times, we admire in Christina the rough, rugged way one can develop around limitations, much the way the trees on Maine's small coastal islands have grown dwarfed, twisted, and beautiful on their windswept land.

WYETH AND THE OLSONS

In the summer of 1939, on his twenty-second birthday, Andrew Wyeth met the Olsons. That day, Wyeth, who summered across the St. George River in Port Clyde with his father, the painter N. C. Wyeth, also met his future wife, Betsy James, who was but seventeen. Betsy had known Alvaro Olson and his sister Christina since she was ten. Having just met Andy, she brought him to the house she once described as "looming up like a weathered ship stranded on a hilltop."

Wyeth discovered two loves that day. In ten months he married Betsy, and together they returned each summer to Cushing, frequently to the Olson home. For years, Wyeth painted the inside of the home and the outside, its occupants and its contents. Eventually, he set up a studio upstairs. One day, having witnessed Christina creeping up the hill from the small graveyard, the idea for his most famous painting came to him.

Christina's World was created in pieces. First Wyeth painted the landscape, then he posed his wife in the grass as a stand-in for Christina. Finally he painted Christina's emaciated arms. Though the painting was not an instant success, Wyeth knew he had uncovered some human essence.

The Wyeths counted the Olsons as their friends; they were never objects of pity. Wyeth calls Christina "a remarkable, austere, intelligent woman" who had a "tremendous knowledge of the history and folklore of her surroundings." Perhaps his feelings for the Olsons are best illuminated in a story Wyeth told reporter Bill Caldwell, a popular writer for the *Portland Press Herald* and *Maine Sunday Telegram* for many years:

> The truth is Christina and her brother Alvaro were both fabulous, wonderful people, with a great grasp of humanity and character. I remember an important and wealthy man who came to talk to me and expressed sympathy toward Christina, calling her a tragic figure. I told him how wrong he was, and that he should go and visit Christina himself and discover how wonderful she was.
>
> A few days later, I was talking with Christina, who mentioned that this well-known man had called to visit her. "What a tragic man" Christina said. "The poor fellow keeps running back to New York and chasing his business. Never knows quite where he belongs or wants to be."

COASTAL COSMOPOLITANS

Located as it is on a point near the tip of a long peninsula, miles from the nearest town and even far from the nearest store, the Olson House appears quite isolated from the rest of the world. But though that may seem true today, it was not in the past. Quite inadvertently, this one house traces the history of the Maine coast and its global connections.

It was built in the late 1700s as a saltwater farm by the Hathorne family, who had first settled on Hathorn Point in 1743 (yes, the spelling changes; and DeLorme's *The Maine Atlas & Gazetteer* spells it "Hawthorne"). It remained in the family, passing from sea captain's son to sea captain's son

until Captain Samuel Hathorne IV, Christina's grandfather, by then retired from the sea, pushed the roof
into a steep pitch, adding a row of bedrooms to
the third story.

The year was 1871, and Captain Hathorne
thereby joined the lucrative summer boarding-
house business. Many who stayed at the
Hathornes' made it an annual visit. Days
would be spent by the shores of Maple Juice
Cove, rowing to nearby islands, getting caught in the fog, or
bound by the tide. Nights would be spent listening to the captain's tales of his life at sea, tales of sailing around Cape
Horn and the Cape of Good Hope, of being captured by
cannibals, and of being shipwrecked three times.

Captain Hathorne finished his sailing life on relatively
quieter runs, sailing brigantines full of ice from the Kennebec River down to the Caribbean, and returning with rum
and spices.

The captain retired, but sailing ships continued. One day,
in 1892, a Swedish sailor by the name of John Olson was
forced ashore by an early freeze on the St. George River.
Soon thereafter John and Kate Hathorne, the captain's
daughter, were married. Christina was born the next year.
Alvaro came a year later, in 1894.

This exotic, cosmopolitan heritage is not apparent in the
Olson House, nor in the paintings of Andrew Wyeth. The
legacy of Christina and Alvaro is of the entrenched Yankee
farmer for whom a trip even to town is a big deal. But Caroline Burr vividly recalls the unusual shells Christina's
mother, Kate, had gathered in the tropics, which the visitors
fondly called "Kate's jewels." Those shells, along with the
stories of exotic adventure, must have also been in
Christina's mind.

There were other Olson children, but the farm passed to
the unmarried brother and sister who did what they could

with the land until they died. Shortly after their deaths, their goods were auctioned off. From sea captain's home to rusticator's haven to immigrant's farm, the house became enough of a celebrity for the rough household tools to sell in 1968 for many times their value. Clam hods, or holders, worth about fifty cents went for $4.50, a wooden ruler went for $5.50. The house was then put on the market. Fearful that it would be torn down, movie producer Joseph E. Levine bought it. He treated it as both monument and museum, installing his own collection of Wyeths inside. Together with Betsy Wyeth, he attempted some needed repairs and slight renovations of the home, removing wallpaper and adding stencils in an effort to reflect the Wyeth vision. But Levine had failed to set off an area for visitor parking and forgot facilities. Neighbors felt their privacy had been invaded, and Levine left with hard feelings.

When the house came up for sale again, Maine coast residents Lee Adams and John Sculley, still flush with a fortune made at Apple Computers, bought it and donated it to the Farnsworth Art Museum in Rockland in 1991.

GETTING TO CUSHING

A visit to the Olson House on its bluff overlooking the St. George River is also a rewarding journey down one of Maine's loveliest peninsulas, home to many local artists as well as fishing folk.

Such a journey could begin in Rockland, where the Farnsworth Museum opened its Wyeth Center in early summer of 1998. Here, in addition to paintings by three generations of Wyeth artists, there is an ongoing look at Andrew Wyeth's methods, comparing a rotating display of his paintings to the drawings that led to them. In its Wyeth Study

Center Wing, the Farnsworth Museum now houses a large body of Andrew Wyeth's papers and drawings, available by appointment.

But it is three miles south, in Thomaston, that the road to Cushing begins. Thomaston is an elegant but strangely shocking town, for classic nineteenth-century architecture is juxtaposed against Maine's only maximum-security prison. Stop in town for café food, or for a visit to the town's several bookstores and its historic mansion Montpelier, which became the setting for *The House of the Seven Gables* after Nathaniel Hawthorne (a distant cousin of the Cushing Hathornes) visited there in 1837. And don't ignore the Maine State Prison Showroom. Prison inmates sell woodwork there made during their free time in hopes of garnering extra cash. The prices are good and the work about as solid as the location it derives from.

Cushing begins about a mile beyond the bridge over the St. George River. About two miles farther, the work of the first of the peninsula's artists makes itself known. A large wooden horse stands proud upon a boulder, backed by a life-size gang of wooden football players. These announce the home where sculptor Bernard Langlais lived before his death in 1977. A moment later, at the bottom of a hill, two mermaid creatures frolic in a small pond. The grounds are private, since Helen Langlais still lives here, but it's hard not to linger, admiring Langlais' artistic enthusiasms. Prophetically, in the early 1970s, Langlais's sculpture of Richard Nixon slowly sank into the mud here.

A. S. FALES & SON

Continuing down the peninsula, stop in at the old, tin-ceilinged A. S. Fales Country Store, which has seen so much traffic over the century and a half of its existence that its wooden floor has already been replaced twice. The store is located at a fork in the road. A small sign notes that the left fork leads to the Olson House. (After one and a half miles, you'll take another left. The Olson House is truly unmistakable.)

Since Fales opened in 1839, the store has been run by six generations of Fales boys. Heather, now in her early twenties, works with her father and grandfather to mark the seventh generation. Though not the oldest family-run general store in Maine (that honor belongs to the Frisbee General Store, in Kittery, which is eleven years senior to Fales and calls itself "North America's oldest family-run store"), Fales is nevertheless a venerable tradition. To many, the store is the center of Cushing.

"Fales' store means Cushing," Betsy Wyeth once explained to a reporter for the *Bangor Daily News*. "If anything ever happened to Fales' store, the heart would go right out of Cushing."

When A. S. Fales & Son first opened, it was located in a converted fishing shack and A. S. ("Elisha") Fales sold his goods to the folks living on the nearby islands. The store was supplied by boat, from the coasters coming up from Boston and Portland; it also sold by boat, to island residents who rowed in for their goods. Later, after the roads came in and Fales moved to its current location, the Fales would make deliveries by horse and then by truck, as many as twenty-five a day. They delivered to the Olsons as well, but because Christina and Alvaro had no phone, a Fales employee would drive over to pick up the order in the morning and come back with it that afternoon.

They don't do house calls today, and there are no longer swarms of men playing cards or arguing politics around the potbellied stove, as poet Ramona Carle Woodbury described in her poem "Along the St. Georges":

Down through the years, Fales' store became the local
  social club.
Around the hot, pot-bellied stove was heard a loud
  hubbub.
Men argued over politics and nearly came to fight
'till John yawned, turned the oil lamp down, and
  bade them all good night.

There also are no longer barrels of crackers and molasses
or people clamoring for Atwood Bitters, but along with gas,
candy, videos, and sandwiches, you'll find shelves piled with
the hip waders used by clam diggers. Come fall, there's
plenty of iridescent orange garb, the mark of hunting season.

Many other artists live in the town of Cushing, population
981. The spot of Andrew Wyeth's coastal home is a well-
guarded secret. Ask for his home at Fales and any number of
people—including at times Andrew Wyeth himself, who
comes to stock up on groceries and visit his friends—will
solemnly shake their heads and say they have no idea where
it's located. Be grateful for the simple no's, though. Richard
Fales insists that "we never send them in the wrong direction, even though we feel like it sometimes." The friendship
is a long one between the Wyeths and the Fales. In the 1960s,
after finishing a painting, Wyeth used to come by and casu-
ally leave it for the folks at the store to view. "'Keep it here
and look it over,' Wyeth would say," according to Richard
Fales. "He'd leave them right on the counter. We wouldn't
advertise, but we would show it to personal friends, if they
were really close."

This spare coastal land of meadows and islands has also
inspired painter Lois Dodd, who turns landscapes into inti-
mate domestic portraits. Dodd lives down the road from the
Olson House. Nearby lives noted gardener and writer Leslie
Land, whose Cushing garden is half the subject of *The 3,000
Mile Garden*, a book and public television program.

Around the cove lives artist Alan Magee. After moving to Maine from New York, Magee gained fame by painting huge, precise renderings of beach stones rubbed smooth by centuries of surf. Magee has since moved into recording more abstract timelessness—childhood memories, dreams, early fears. Nearby are the homes of photographer John Paul Caponigro, son of another famous photographer, Paul Caponigro. These artists have continued to keep Cushing known in an international arena. The work of most of them can be found at the Farnsworth Museum.

To see memories of Cushing from an earlier time, visit the Cushing Historical Society Museum on the same road as the Olson House, open during the summer by appointment only. The focus here is on Cushing's colonial history, when this area, like most of the coast, was a place of frequent skirmishes between English settlers and Native Americans, as well as between the English and the French. There are a few glass cases with household and agricultural items, maps, paintings, and a small library.

Places to See, Eat, and Stay

Cap'n Frost Bed and Breakfast, Thomaston: (207) 354-8217.

Cushing Historical Society Museum, open seasonally by appointment: (207) 354-0430, or call Fales Store for assistance.

A. S. Fales & Son Country Store: (207) 354-6431.

Farnsworth Art Museum, Rockland: (207) 596-6457.

Harbor View Restaurant, Thomaston: (207) 354-8173.

Maine State Prison Showroom, Thomaston: (207) 354-2535, ext. 272.

Maine Watercraft Museum, open seasonally, Thomaston: (207) 354-0444.

Montpelier—the General Henry Knox Museum, open seasonally, Thomaston: (207) 354-8062.

Neville Antiques: (207) 354-8055.

Olson House, open seasonally: (207) 354-0102 or (207) 596-6457.

Thomaston Cafe and Bakery, Thomaston: (207) 354-8589.

Thomaston Books & Prints, Thomaston: (207) 354-0001 or (800) 300-3008.

5

ROADSIDE HISTORY
IN WHITEFIELD

(STATE ROUTES 194 AND 126, ABOUT NINE MILES
EAST OF GARDINER, OR TWELVE MILES NORTHWEST
OF WISCASSET)

Like a pop-up guide, the stories of the central Maine town of Whitefield can be read in slender segments while traveling down any of its roads. The pages? Utility poles, those roadside fixtures so familiar they're usually barely noticed. But along Whitefield's State Routes 126, 194, 218, the Townhouse Road, and especially the Carlton Road (also known as Hollywood Boulevard), these poles have become a treasure map to the history of this town southeast of the state capitol in Augusta. You can't miss them.

Decked with boldly bright images painted by local fourth- and fifth-grade students, the poles are chapters in the greater Whitefield story. On the intersection of State 218 and State 194, a man dressed in black stands on a rooftop, wrestling the Devil. Scrawled print nearby explains how the Devil came to hear the words of the evangelical Reverend George Whitefield. Summoning him to a wrestling match, the reverend pushed the Devil off the steeple, and the Devil was never seen again. None of this happened locally, but the glory of it inspired a change in the town's name from Balltown to Whitefield.

Near the Grange Hall up on Grand Army Hill (State 126), another pole illustrates scenes from the Grange movement. Since the Hall was built by Civil War veterans, it also tells of the war, of the 117 who fought and the dozen who paid three hundred dollars so as not to fight.

Down the road from the Grange Hall stands a pole celebrating the old tradition of hanging a May basket, along with step-by-step instructions on how to make and hang one. It's a stealth kind of activity we are told, for the instructions end with, "If the person inside catches you they can kiss you."

On Townhouse Road, the road that parallels both the Sheepscot River and State 218, cows graze on a striking glacial moraine. When milking time comes, the cows halt traffic as they loll across the road. Accordingly, one pole shows farm scenes, another farm life, or more precisely, what people used to do before television. This pole focuses on the game suppers once held at the Union Hall. In this child's-eye view of the suppers, a chicken drives its own wagon to the hall where a kangaroo, whale, and rattlesnake mingle. There's also a public golf driving range here, reminding us that while Whitefield has been a rural farm community, it is now becoming a suburb to Augusta.

The force behind the paintings is Natasha Mayers, an activist community artist who engaged students at the Whitefield Elementary School to help with the ideas and the painting. While she has worked with communities around the world on many a mural, to Mayers' knowledge—and to the knowledge of officials at Central Maine Power, the local power company who approved the use of their poles for paintings— hers are the only utility poles used as canvases anywhere in the nation.

TOWN ACTIVITIES

If you plan to visit Whitefield, population 1,900, you might have a hard time finding it. You might even have a hard time spotting it on the map, for many maps still divide Whitefield from North Whitefield. Both now form the town of Whitefield.

Go there and you'll find a little grocery store with gas pumps (marked by a pole about the old Whitefield general store, with the announcement, "it sold everything from rubber boots to harnesses"). The school and church are on State 126, the town hall is on the Townhouse Road, and there's not much else that looks public, except for signs announcing homegrown products. On State 126, at Blueberry Hill Farm, just over the Whitefield line in Jefferson, you'll find Ellis Percy selling maple syrup, pickled garlic, fiddleheads, and the world's crispiest dilly bean, or so a neighbor claims. Recently, the Sheepscot Valley Brewing Company opened a microbrewery on Townhouse Road. There are also a few bed-and-breakfasts, including one at Percy's Blueberry Hill Farm, where you'll find fields of blueberries in season. The other is on Townhouse Road, run by local historian David Chase. But there's no public place to sit and eat in town. For that you'll have to stop in Gardiner, Hallowell, Damariscotta, Newcastle, or Wiscasset.

Such an odd assortment of activities is typical of rural Maine towns, especially those with little access to tourism, though the particular bent of Whitefield—homemade and homegrown—may be more common of the back-to-the-landers than is typical of other Maine towns, for many came to Whitefield in the 1960s and 1970s attracted by the rolling farmland and low real estate costs. But scratch other sleepy rural Maine towns and you'll find a similar eclectic array of enterprises. No other town, however, proclaims its history right on its roads. It is the poles that now most distinguish Whitefield, centering it around a hub of other rural activities.

Like canoeing. The Sheepscot River, running from Sheepscot Pond on State 3 in Palermo through Long Pond, then through Coopers Mills, Whitefield, and Head Tide to Sheepscot Bay below Wiscasset, is a celebrated river trip. Writes canoe guide Eben Thomas in *Canoeing Maine #2*, "It is hard to believe a twelve mile trip of this magnitude is available in central Maine, but it is!" The most popular place to put in, according to Thomas as well as DeLorme's *The Maine Atlas & Gazetteer*, is at State 126 in Whitefield, five hundred yards west of the general store. You can easily canoe as far as Head Tide, passing a pool that can turn black with alewives and lampreys at the spring tide. This leg is considered a good river for learning white-water skills. You can also continue your trip from Head Tide to Wiscasset, passing the lovely, nineteenth-century hamlet of Sheepscot, where you'll find reversing falls. Read a canoeing guide first, however. Each leg has one portage.

Near the bridge at the junction of State 218 and State 194, there's another sort of artwork, the metal, weblike intricacies of sculptor Roger Majorowicz, including his *Jawmill*. It's part shark, part sawmill, and it screeches like a vicious mechanized animal when you turn it. While Majorowicz can use simple, store-bought metal for his work, he frequently creates his sculptural assemblies from old tools, even old farm tractors.

You can also take a hike. The Carlton Road, or Hollywood Boulevard, was formerly known as Mast Road. This was the first road in town, carved during the French and Indian wars, and used for dragging masts south to Boston. There's a public game preserve here, a favorite of locals for cross-country skiing and hiking.

WHITEFIELD: CENTRAL TO CENTRAL MAINE

South of Whitefield, State 218 and State 194 come together again at Head Tide, or Head of Tide, a two hundred-year-old village at the Sheepscot River's head of the tide—the farther reach of tidal waters in a river. With fourteen structures on the National Register of Historic Places and a marker at the birthplace of poet Edward Arlington Robinson, winner of several Pulitzer prizes and author of the well-known poem "Richard Cory," this place has barely been encroached upon by the modern world, except through the shouts of those swimming at the Head Tide dam.

Due west from Head Tide, on State 218 in Dresden, stands the Pownalborough Court House, a pre-Revolutionary building housing Maine's oldest standing court house. It was built in 1761 for settlers who would otherwise need to travel to Boston for legal business. This being one of the earliest attempts of self-government among settlers in the New World, it offered a chance for law and order to flourish in the wild woods that were becoming settled, in this area, by an array of Harvard-educated men.

In addition to the courtroom, the courthouse also held a tavern and living quarters for the judge on the third floor. Today there's a museum about the ice trade downstairs. Before refrigeration, ice cut from the Kennebec and Sheepscot Rivers was taken down to the Caribbean, where it iced everything from drinks to meats. The neighboring cemetery is from the Revolutionary War. The courthouse is a rare place to spend some time. Afterwards, walk the nature trails along the river and ponder the thoughts of those creating a new nation.

To the east lies Jefferson, at the northern tip of lovely Damariscotta Lake. Keep driving and you get to the town of Washington, which has Luce's Bargain Shop, one of those great secondhand stores with just enough disarray to keep you plowing through it, sure of a fabulous find down the next aisle.

Then, due north in Coopers Mills, is the ultimate Maine antique and junk emporium, the not-to-be-missed Elmer's Barn. Nineteenth-century satin gowns mix with boxes of nails and screws. Rooms fill with pianos, desks, and bed frames, more rooms are piled with books, old art, dishes, tools, and who knows what else. This is the quintessential secondhand store, capped by a larger-than-life chainsaw sculpture of the T-shirted Elmer rising from a mass of portals, window frames, clawfoot tubs, and stacks of simple junk. The barn itself is worth a trip to the region.

WHITEFIELD PEOPLE

But first, drive around this rather dispersed town; or better, take a bicycle out on its quiet, winding roads. In their meanderings, Whitefield's roads are the picture of rural life, passing through deep fields and gardens, classic farmhouses, and a scattering of trailers. Much of the life visible from the road bespeaks rural contentment, and a kind of mixed employment based on the land and on outside work, also not uncommon a century ago. That's the life Millie and Onofrio Sabatine had, making cheese in an old farmhouse down one of these roads.

With dried flowers hanging from the rafters of the pre-revolutionary farmhouse and a ten-gallon pot resting on the wood-burning stove, the place looks as if the Sabatines had been making their mozzarella, provolone, and parmesan in that very home for generations. But Millie's cheesemaking was an art of only twenty-two years' duration in Maine, about thirty-two years in all.

"I take about half evening milk and half morning milk," the pleasant-faced, motherly woman explains one summer day while resting in the sitting room that lies off her kitchen. "Then I heat it to about ninety degrees, add a starter and rennet—"

"Don't give away any trade secrets," husband Onofrio cautions, only half in jest. His wife just smiles. The process became so ingrained in her muscles, she literally couldn't remember all the secrets she would need to give away were someone to make her mozzarella.

Summers, Millie Sabatine used to make about fifteen pounds of mozzarella daily from the fifteen or sixteen gallons of milk their six cows produce. Come fall, Onofrio would welcome the cool weather by bundling up the dried corn-stalks from his garden into rows of slender tepees. It's the way his Italian grandfather did it, and people from all over would come to photograph the unusual beauty of his rows of bound stalks.

Come winter, Millie's cheese took longer to set, and so she would work her mozzarella only three days a week. Then she made hard cheese—the more time-consuming aged pro-volone and parmesan, which also lasted much longer. The parmesan must be salted periodically, and oil and vinegar added.

The Sabatines couldn't travel much with their cheese mak-ing, but with the cycles of their life, milking cows at morning and evening, heating and wringing cheese according to the heat of the day, they had plenty of time for visitors. A visitor marvels at the ancient nature of this rhythmic day, saying, "Very few people live a life so . . ."

"Chained?" Millie laughs.

Chained no longer. As of fall of 1997, the Sabatines sold their cows and have retired to a more liberated life.

Off the Vigue Road, working in a small room pinned to a large barn, you'll find upholsterer Barbara Meyer, likely with nails in her mouth and a small hammer in her hand. Pretty normal stuff of the trade. But Meyer's couches are not normal, not for the late twentieth century. Increasingly, her pieces are covered with organic cottons and stuffed with compostable battings. Indeed, one of her favorite new stuffings is a garden mulch made of waste wool and camel hair, which she discovered in a gardening magazine. EweMulch, as it is known, turned out to be a lot like a wool batting she's found inside old chairs but not on the market.

This pioneering work into nontoxic, environmentally sound furniture is one side of Meyer's business. The other side is her fantasy chairs. They may have wings on them— true wings, perhaps with feathers—or a head, or carved hooves. For several years now, Meyer has been experimenting with making sculptural chairs like the one she calls "Pig Chair," upholstered in pink satin, complete with angel wings and pink hooves. The chair is a tribute to a pet pig the family called Lord Fauntleroy, until, that is, they called him bacon.

HISTORY

As you continue your drive around Whitefield, pull off the road (carefully); peer at the poles. The history they portray, their humor and pathos, reflects Whitefield and the struggle and satisfaction of rural Maine life. They also remind us that

what we see is never all there is. Quiet Whitefield, we discover, once had a hospital, sidewalks, a dance hall, even a
train station and a railway leading to the coast.

Granted, it wasn't the best train line. Called the Wiscasset, Waterville and Farmington Line, or the WW&F, it was a
narrow-gauge rail dubbed the Milky Way for its freight of
dairy products, and the Weak, Weary and Feeble for
its reputation. A pole marks the site of the old
station, near the post office on Route 126. Until
1933, when it took one final tumble, the train also
took students from the eighteen lower schools scattered throughout Whitefield down to Wiscasset
for high school.

Today, what was railroad is but a flatbed,
turned into a pleasant walking, or cross-country
skiing, trail that follows the Sheepscot River for about a mile
to a nice little bridge. You can get to it at Clary Mill on State
218 between Coopers Mills and the Superette in Whitefield.
How will you know Clary Mill? By the pole that features the
old sawmill, of course.

Whitefield was settled by stubborn Liberty Men, who
cleared and cultivated the land and refused to give it up to
the actual owners, the wealthy Kennebec Proprietors who
came back after the Revolutionary War to claim their
territory.

Dressed as Indians, the Liberty Men set fire to Tory
sawmills and enacted other acts of guerrilla warfare against
the Proprietors, some of whom were descendants of the pioneering group of the Pownalborough courthouse. These
names still suggest ownership in Maine: Mr. Hallowell, Mr.
Gardiner, Mr. Pitts, Mr. Vassall, Mr. Vaughan, and Mr. Bow-
doin. On the bottom of the pole that marks this history, the
Proprietors are painted in fancy dress. On the top is the dec-
laration, "This is our land. We won't pay the Kennebec
Proprietors."

The town was later populated by Irish immigrants who came here before the 1846 potato famine. In 1833, White-field had the largest Catholic community in Maine—a thousand people. You know this by another pole, standing in front of the St. Denis Church, built in 1818, the second oldest Catholic church in New England. On the pole, which is marked with shamrocks and Celtic crosses, are the reasons why the Irish left: "No vote, no schools, no religious freedom." Look around the cemetery beside the church; the hopes and pathos of these early immigrants are easily imagined.

CAN ART HEAL COMMUNITY WOUNDS?

Natasha Mayers's idea for the massive pole project has its base in rural Maine life. It begins not as community outreach but as simple maternal ingenuity. One summer day in the early 1980s, tired of having children underfoot, Mayers sent her son Noah and a friend outside to paint. "What should we paint?" the boys clamored. "Why not paint that pole out there?" the mother answered. It was, in fact, a driveway utility pole. End of Chapter 1. Chapter 2 begins ten years later. Whitefield had been ravaged by a major battle over school funding, causing a bitter rift between those who wanted to cap property taxes (thereby also slashing the school budget) and those who wanted the school budget to stand, regardless of the tax cost.

The tax caps did pass, with the result that the roof of the school began leaking, spreading physical damage. Two principals quit in swift succession, as did a secretary and numerous classroom teachers, among them a nationally honored science teacher who had brought the town thousands of dollars in grant money. In the wake of this struggle, Mayers pondered her role as a community artist. Could art heal the community's wounds?

"This was the number-one reason, the most, most, most important reason for doing the telephone poles," Mayers says. "I was thinking, 'What could I do with art to make the town love its kids, to see how important the school is? What could my contribution be?' I was looking to find the sweetest, most satisfying gift to help the healing process."

As she talks, Mayers is sitting in the kitchen of the house she helped build, a room crowded with books, art from innumerable friends, and rows of plates painted by her children. Her eyes wander through the window to her yard outside and fix on the painted utility pole. After a decade, the painting had faded only a little. Looking at the pole, her idea clicked.

Mayers called the local power company. She called the school. She called some friends well-versed in local history. By October of that year, poles were getting painted.

Chapter 3 to the story opened in 1996, with the town rescinding the cap and a shaken community taking a look at itself. What they find are feisty, independent people—they're descendants of Liberty Men and Irish Catholics, after all—people who want to uphold the way of life for which they believe Maine stands. To some, that life is focused on children and their future, harking back to the very first town meeting, in 1810, when the town raised four hundred dollars for its schools. To others, that life is focused on liberty, and part of liberty is power over one's money. Unlike other issues in Maine, this is not a question of those "from away" versus native Mainers. The education of children falls on both sides of the question.

But this tax battle does reflect a change in the entire economic structure of the nation. There are fewer and fewer manual jobs, even in Maine. No longer can Maine children be educated through eighth grade and expect to find a job in the mill, or on the farm or even cutting timber. In Maine, as in California or Rhode Island, children need to think as well as till, to question as well as remember.

The healing over Whitefield's tax conflict will take time. Whether the poles have helped is a question left to the decades. For now, they have linked memories across generations, through engaging children in the town's own myths, and engraving the stories for all to read and continually remember. Besides, the stories are great. There's the one of Kate Morse, who at age fifty-eight, in the early part of this century, started a cottage hospital on the Townhouse Road. No one was turned away, not even a burn victim who needed nine months of care and hadn't a cent to his name. The site of the hospital, once a smokehouse, now a microbrewery, is marked by a pole featuring nurses and a child's rendition of an eye chart that reads:

C O
T T A
G E H O
S P I T A L

The young students who created the poles have gained a way to make their mark in town, a mark they see daily. Perhaps student Andrew Harris, speaking from the combined fourth and fifth grade class at Whitefield Elementary School, sums it up best. He worked on the Liberty Men pole. "I liked learning about the Liberty Men and how they burned the barns and terrorized the mappers [surveyors]," he says. "It looks really neat. I like the fact that when I'm pretty old, my grandchildren will be able to see them." His enthusiasm causes Mayers to grin. Though the paintings may last years, they are by no means permanent.

Places to See, Eat, and Stay

Blueberry Hill Farm: (207) 549-7448.

Chase Bed and Breakfast: (207) 549-5761.

Elmer's Barn, State Route 17, Coopers Mills: (207) 549-7671.

Luce's Bargain Shop, Washington: (207) 845-2420.

Old Head Tide Church, Head Tide.

Pownalborough Court House, Dresden: (207) 882-6817.

Sheepscot Valley Brewing Company, Townhouse Road: (207) 549-5530.

6

ISLAND RHYTHMS OF CARVERS HARBOR, VINALHAVEN

(MAINE STATE FERRY SERVICE FROM ROCKLAND, ON U.S. ROUTE 1)

Stand close to the bow of the ferry as you enter Vinal-haven's Reach. From there, nothing can distract you from the stunning serenade of tree, rock, and sea. As island follows island, boulder seems to tumble over boulder to rest on blue-green water. Above, stately groves of spruce seek the sky. Watch as granite cliffs yield to fields of yellow hay, and lone farmhouses give way to the rush of Vinalhaven's sole town, Carvers Harbor. Here homes extend out into the harbor on wharves, while others push into the Reach from islands and craggy, crablike points of land surrounding the harbor.

On my last journey through this enchanted passage, taken on the stalwart, rumbling, ungainly ferry named The Governor Curtis, I overheard an old sailor muttering something. "What?" I ventured. "Prettiest spot in Maine," he repeated.

From the visitor's perspective, at least, this beauty couldn't have happened to a nicer people. Hospitality is a long-standing tradition on the island. A hundred years ago, an account described the people of Vinalhaven as "noted for their humanity and benevolence to strangers." Even in town, drivers patiently wait for tourists to amble across the street, and routinely raise one hand off the steering wheel to signal friend and visitor alike with Maine's laconic wave.

With a population of but 1,053 year-round (which triples or even quadruples in the summer), people on Vinalhaven clearly matter. This is especially true for its children. At graduation each year, at least one-quarter of the town turns out to watch the rather diminutive ceremonies. The 1998 graduates numbered eight.

PORTRAIT OF AN AUTHOR AS AN ENVIRONMENTAL DISASTER

My own gauge of the cordiality of Vinalhaven became etched into granite—or perhaps mud—via a couple of mishaps. The first was the day I decided to go exploring in our Jeep Cherokee in the middle of mud season. I drove out of Carvers Harbor, heading in a northeasterly direction, seeking the surf of open ocean. When the road ended in a driveway, I took a promising trail to my left, oblivious to the mud beneath my wheels and to the rather private nature of this path. I was looking up, admiring some towering spruce trees when I found my wheels caught tight.

Oh yes, I tried. I shifted into four-wheel drive, then four-wheel drive low. I braced the wheels with branches and wood planks, then entire logs. After rutting the path forever, I'm afraid, I grabbed my little boy, two years old at the time and fast asleep through all my grinding and stick jumping, and trudged off for help.

The closest home was a magnificent yellow farmhouse, the kind that has extension after extension, going on forever. A woman answered the door. Matter-of-factly, as if she had been expecting the visit, she piled Daniel and me into her truck to survey the trouble. We were back in a minute; her hefty truck would not do. Daniel was still asleep when we returned to the scene in her tractor.

With perfect Yankee discretion, my valiant rescuer loaded us into her tractor and eased it down to the Jeep, still up to its belly in mud. Only after pulling me out and offering a hose to splash the mud from the car did she tell me the landowners were probably watching out their front window high on a hill. Then she poured a few fingers of whiskey in a chipped glass to quiet my nerves. I must have spent an hour nestled in the bay of her kitchen window listening to island stories, while Daniel, who awakened only after all the hefting and grinding was over, played with the shells she had spread out along the windowsill. Never once did she let out what a fool I had been. When I returned the next year, I realized to my eternal shame that what I had driven through really was but a path and a private one at that, no road at all. My excuse was that I was suffering the shock, and perhaps the liberation, of enforced separation.

Which brings up another aspect of visiting Vinalhaven—the ferry. This particular trip to Vinalhaven happened to be an overnight family outing just at the onset of spring fever. It was also, as we discovered, the final weekend of school vacation. We were only going overnight, but Bill and I piled everything we could into and onto the Jeep—bikes, books, bags, even a canoe. On Sunday, we blithely rolled our car into line for the ferry, only to find that we were three cars away from getting on the last ferry. We hoped. We worried. We waited. Perhaps some of the cars were really in line for the Monday morning ferry. Perhaps they'd squeeze in tight. Perhaps someone would change their mind. The ferry smoked in. The cars rolled on. There was a bit more room. Two more cars got on. Not us.

There's always plenty of room for people on the ferry; it's car space that's scarce. Since Bill had to teach in the morning, he walked on, preparing to hitch home. My schedule being somewhat looser (and Daniel's schedule being nonexistent), we stayed behind with the car, which was now first in line for Monday's ferry. For a moment, Daniel and I stood on the dock, waving as if we were separating across a wide ocean, then I went on to seed my oats—right into the mud.

As to managing the ferry, there are a limited number of reserved spots for cars (for a small surcharge); otherwise, there are elaborate rules for getting your car in line (and moving it up each time the ferry comes). Get an islander to explain that part to you, but bear in mind that without reservations you might find yourself spending a weekend on Vinalhaven obsessed by getting off it. If you're coming only for a short stay, think about bringing bikes only and leaving your car in Rockland. It's cheaper. Bring bikes, or plan to rent them on the island.

WELCOMING INTERLOPERS

Our second Vinalhaven mishap occurred one Sunday night after we had sailed into Carvers Harbor in our own boat. We obtained a mooring and spent an hour or two admiring the view from the harbor, watching the sky turn an early pink while a thunderstorm spilled somewhere west of us. Though we had food on board, we decided to go to town for a feast at the Sand Dollar, greedy for their huge portions (unfortunately, this great restaurant has since closed). Donning our yellow slickers, we rowed through a swarm of mosquitoes, spent a moment watching fishermen high on a pier over the harbor, and walked a block or so of downtown. Not a restaurant was open.

We stopped at a little general store instead. Then the lights went on in The Haven across the street. While Bill popped over, visions of their elegant food swirled through my stomach. "They're having an art opening," he reported. We hit that opening with all the vehemence of starved sailors, though feeling a little weird that all were well-dressed while the three of us were prominently in our yellow rain gear. And it was surprising how few were even glancing at the art on the walls, and how large a level of formality there was for an opening. Wine and beer were brought out on little trays, and though there was a table spread with hors d'oeuvres, there were many more trays going around with more food. After about fifteen minutes of trying to restrain ourselves from eating everything, a tall slender woman came up to us. "Are you wondering what's going on here?" she asked, with extreme discretion. "It's an art opening," replied Bill, his certainty almost aggressive. "Actually, it's a wedding," she countered. "But you're welcome to stay." Sheepishly, we declined the hospitality and had dinner on the boat.

AN ISLAND OF PRESERVES

With bikes or strong legs, there's much to do on Vinalhaven without a car. Pick up a copy of the island brochure, a document that focuses on where you can be rather than what you can buy. The town has conserved its land into sixteen parks or preserves on Vinalhaven and its surrounding islands; several are within walking distance, more within an easy biking distance. One of them has the following directions: bear right at the cola-bottle-statue-of-liberty. You'll know it when you see it.

If people matter in Vinalhaven, so does the land and its structures. At roughly seven miles by five, Vinalhaven is the largest island in Maine without a bridge to the mainland. Its spruce woods alternate with moorlands and great granite outcroppings much the way the islands alternate with water. No two vistas are alike. All are spectacular, whether the vista be of a drowned forest turned into a swamp of spindly driftwood, the solitary Fox Islands Thorofare lighthouse at the foot of a sweeping hill, or a lone tree on an island in the mouth of some miniature bay.

Most important about Vinalhaven, or any Maine island, is that you don't need to go far to be overwhelmed by wonder. It is the quiet moments that are most memorable, those witnessed at close range, like the special beauty of an entrance to lush, moss-covered woods, weathered logs and dirt paths arranged as if by an enchanted gardener, the velvet of thick, pink moss under bare feet.

Frequently such moments are mirrored by large pools—abandoned quarries left from the booming stone quarrying industry at the end of the last century—and nourished by blueberries, blackberries, and raspberries sprouting along the paths. Now filled with water, several quarries have become public swimming holes; Lawson's is a mile from downtown, Booth's 1.6 miles. Even closer to town, behind the medical center, Armbrust Hill Town Park boasts a playground as well as an extensive trail of wildflowers and native plants looping around a large quarry.

But if you've only time to visit one place, go to Lane's Island Nature Conservancy Preserve, reached by crossing a picturesque bridge to Lane's Island, a fifteen-minute walk from the ferry. You enter the preserve at Indian Creek, where an inlet empties to a calm lakelike sea at ebb tide and fills to pounding surf at its flow. Masses of ground shells indicate the ancient presence of Native Americans. A seaside walk through fields that have the sweeping feel of moors leads to a high cliff. Open ocean ends at open sky, with a hint of the offshore island of Matinicus deep on the horizon. On a hot summer day, crickets chirp in the dry grass, vying with the surf. This is why you have come to the island.

CARVERS HARBOR

Carvers Harbor, Vinalhaven's one town, is a small, casual place, barely changed in appearance from turn-of-the-century photographs. Though age and disaster have taken their toll, most of the street is still composed of old frame buildings, two and three stories high.

There's the mustard and brown fire station, a hardware store to get lost in, a few gift shops and a handful of restaurants, including one located in an old pharmacy, complete with tin walls and classic shelves.

The Haven, where the three strange sailors were welcomed into a wedding, is the "fancy restaurant" of town, where islanders take their moms for Mother's Day and their children for graduation. There's art on the walls, but if there seems to be a party inside, it's more likely a wedding reception than an art opening!

We often visit Vinalhaven off-season, so we stay at the Tidewater Motel, which is open year-round. Built on a bridge over a causeway, the tide rises and falls beneath your room, recalling the magic feeling of being cradled in a boat in a harbor. If you ask, the staff will attempt to reserve a space for your car on the ferry. They have bikes for rent for both adults and children.

The town's most intriguing structure is the Odd Fellows Hall, now elegantly painted in gray, black, and gilt, its window displays strangely musty. This curious building has been the home and studio of artist Robert Indiana since 1978. The windows are a study of black humor, frequently featuring skulls, bones, and odd ducks. They serve as a kind of warning, too. Indiana relishes his privacy; he does not like visitors knocking at his door.

Until recently, an elderly woman down the street had taken on the artist, mounting her own more sentimental, miniature displays. Her window sported an elaborate wooden dollhouse with a china hen watching a miniature television while an old bunny rested in a dark rocking chair. But now Marie, as a Vinalhaven acquaintance explained, "is no longer with us and her windows are bare, at least until some other creative soul moves in."

THE WORKING FISHERY

For a downtown, Carvers Harbor seems unusually easygoing. At other Maine harbors, especially those with a sense of remoteness, frustrations are frequently expressed in driving. On Vinalhaven, the leisurely, communal nature of islands remains, despite any sense of claustrophobia. At least that's what we've felt. Children ride bikes, teenagers lounge near take-out stands, tourists watch the harbor, and cars seem to amble down the road. Vinalhaven people protest this characterization. "We have our share of frustrated local drivers," says one resident. In the afternoon, the harbor is likely to be filled with fishing boats, but few boats wait out the morning at anchor. Vinalhaven is a working fishery.

It is frequently distinguished on this score from North Haven, its northerly neighbor. Broadly speaking, North Haven shelters more cruisers and summer millionaires. Anne Morrow Lindbergh's family had a home on North Haven; when Charles visited, he landed a seaplane on the Thorofare. The Saltonstalls and the Cabots also summer there. Vinalhaven keeps the fishing folk, or so it is said. A peek at Vinalhaven from across the Fox Islands Thorofare reveals that Vinalhaven, too, has its share of imposing summer homes.

To those who grew up on Vinalhaven, the grass frequently seems greener on North Haven. A young woman who grew up on the island told me that many kids long for the broader reaches of North Haven, where there's more art in the schools, more to do in the summers.

I've only been to North Haven in summer, and the comparison I make is to a miniature Nantucket, where elegantly coifed women in shorts and sandals greet the ferry accompanied by children who manage to remain spotless even after visiting the ice-cream stand. As an indication of its exclusivity, North Haven offers very few places to eat and only one place to stay, the idea being that you have your own place and get invited to the round of social events on the island. Vinalhaven has a handful of summer guest houses and a pageful of restaurants; after a hard day of work, it's nice sometimes to grab a crabroll and sit on the dock. There are at least three galleries on North Haven; Vinalhaven has but one, the Fog Gallery, featuring local artists, both year-round and summer people. Again, Vinalhaven is the working island. Artists live and work here. Indiana is the most well-known. Come summer, more Portland-based artists, among them Katarina Weslien, Alison Hildreth, and photographer Christopher Ayres move in, with many more coming to the

Vinalhaven Press, a sort of artist's retreat for printmakers, funded in part by the proceeds of their work.

The Vinalhaven Press was established in 1984 by Pat Nick, an island daughter who was raised in Boston in winter and Vinalhaven in summer. She spent years as an arts administrator. Then, while attending a conference on transforming old school buildings into artists' retreats, she realized that she had the perfect building right in Vinalhaven. Within a year, she opened the press, inviting artists to come to the island for two weeks at a time, putting them up in the home she restored on Lane's Island. The artists get uninterrupted time to work and the assistance of master printers. Their families get an island retreat for a few weeks. Nick then markets a limited edition of their work, splitting the proceeds. But though the Vinalhaven Press has made a name for the island in the art world, the operation remains low-key.

HISTORY

Vinalhaven was an early fishing island. Because of the foxes seen flitting around the island, in 1603 Europeans named it South Fox Island. Its twin, North Haven, was known as North Fox Island. Though later renamed for John Vinyl, Esquire, of Boston, the waters that divide the two islands retain the old name, Fox Islands Thorofare.

The islands were known to Maine's Native Americans for their fisheries and clams. They jealously guarded the islands, first by canoe, and later, after capturing some white sailors and forcing some sailing instruction, in sailing vessels they had seized from the British. In 1724, according to historian Dean Snow of the State University of New York, fifty canoes of Wabanaki Indians captured a fleet of twenty-two British vessels. They sailed the vessels up the St. George River in an attempt to storm the British fort there, but were unsuccessful.

By the 1760s, David Wooster established the first permanent European settlement. But during the American Revolution, when the British held Castine, the Tories swooped down, raided the island, burnt its buildings, and impressed the islanders to work on British fortifications. Castine and Vinalhaven, remember, may be hours apart by car and ferry, but by water, only a few nautical miles separate them.

Another famous nautical Vinalhaven story occurred in 1836, when the ship the *Royal Tar* took shelter in Vinalhaven after encountering a storm on its way from Boston to Canada. On the boat were crew, passengers, and a circus. When the ship caught fire, most of the humans were rescued; the animals could not be saved. Days later, the carcasses of an elephant and tigers, leopards, lions, and camels washed ashore on nearby islands.

With its mostly rocky soil, Vinalhaven has never been much of a farming island. Its two industries have been fishing and quarrying. During the mid-nineteenth century, some seventy-five vessels on both the Fox Islands brought in codfish to thirteen local curing yards. The salt cod was sent to Boston, keeping four freighters busy with the task. But in the late nineteenth century quarries eclipsed the fisheries.

Stonecutters came from Italy, Britain, and Scandinavia, with the Italians being the most numerous and notorious. Stories of Italian stonecutters—with their vibrant songs, boccie tournaments, and Socialist demands—are still told today on the island. Vinalhaven provided the stone for the Boston Museum of Fine Arts and the huge pillars for the Cathedral of St. John the Divine in New York City. One Vinalhaven company alone, Governor Bodwell, employed as many as fifteen hundred people, more than live on the entire island today.

The industry soared during the nation's building boom after the Civil War. Hurricane Island, behind Greens Island off the southwest shores of Vinalhaven, had a large town, with as many as one thousand stonecutters. The European stonecutters had homes, a school, and a dance hall. Because the island is dry, when the stonecutters weren't out cutting and carving they made frequent use of visiting ships as floating bars.

The industry collapsed in the early 1930s, when poured cement and steel framing became both popular and economical. Hurricane Island closed down in a matter of days, the workers leaving homes, belongings, even tables set for dinner. Today, Hurricane Island is the home of the popular Outward Bound School, dedicated to helping people discover the self-confidence and ecological awareness garnered from learning how to survive in the wilderness. Open boats of Hurricane Island students can be seen rowing over Penobscot Bay; some are on their way to solo experiences on the Penobscot Bay islands.

With quarrying lost, Vinalhaven reverted to fishing. It still is a fishing community that accepts but doesn't cater to its summer people. The island has one school encompassing all grades, a lumber yard, Claw Island Foods (which cooks and freezes eight tons of lobster daily to send to markets across the United States, the Far East, and Europe), two trucking companies, two groceries, a hospice, a medical center, an auto repairman, six lobster dealers, and 280 folk with lobster licenses.

Places to See, Eat, and Stay

Candlepin Lodge: (207) 863-2730.

Fox Islands Inn: (207) 863-2122.

The Haven: (207) 863-4969.

The Harbor Gawker: (207) 863-9365.

The Islander: (207) 863-2028.

Lane's Island Nature Conservancy Preserve (no phone).

Libby House: (207) 863-4696.

Maine State Ferry Service

  Vinalhaven: (207) 863-4421.

  Rockland: (207) 596-2203.

Payne Homestead: (207) 863-9963.

Surfside: (207) 863-2767.

Tidewater Motel: (207) 863-4618.

Vinalhaven Historical Society Museum: (207) 863-4410.

7
ADDISON
DREAMERS

(ADDISON ROAD, THREE MILES SOUTH OF
COLUMBIA FALLS)

It is possible to take a more direct route to Addison, leaving U.S. 1 at what seems like an improbably placed mall at the summit of a hill near Columbia Falls. (I'm sure, however, the placement makes sense to those who live nearby.) But when I go to this part of the world, I prefer to elude the modern era as much as possible, so I snake my way there, leaving U.S. Route 1 just after Harrington, following a dirt road cut through to Addison from Marshville. Either way, the road reaches the same spot, sweeping into town over the West Branch of the Pleasant River as it meanders its way to Pleasant Bay.

I have been through Addison several times in recent years. Each visit, I find myself astounded by the quiet, ancient beauty here, a grand stillness that makes the chirping of crickets seem clamorous. The peninsulas east of Gouldsboro, in the area best defined as down east, seem older, more weathered, than the rest of Maine, as if vinyl siding and twentieth century technology had passed them by. But there is something even more in Addison: a vision so improbable that even now, part of me believes it to be a mirage.

At a bend in the Addison Road, at a spot where road and river meet in a luminous green marsh, stand the thick dark ribs of a wooden schooner under construction. At first glance, I assume these immense ribs, looking something like the skeleton of a wooly mammoth, are the wreck of an old boat rescued from the deep. Then I drive closer, close enough to hear the lonely rasp of the builder, and I realize this is not a reconstruction; this is the real thing.

A century ago, the sight of a schooner being built at the edge of Maine's circuitous coast would have been about as unusual a fixture as a gas station is today. But at the end of the second millennium, it is safe to say that builder Dino Fonda is alone in spending his days hammering away on a massive schooner in an old Maine boatyard. Well, not quite alone: "It's the Lord and I," he says.

Fonda, however, is not alone in coming to these windswept shores with a mission. I've just barely scratched the surface of Addison, population 1,114, but I find in this town of tall, weathered Greek Revival homes, its yards running wild with roses, more than a few who have come to live out a dream.

Over sixty years ago, the great watercolorist John Marin went searching for the American land. He found his vision of it at the tip of Addison, a region of South Addison known as Cape Split. More recently, daughter-in-law Norma Marin took on the formidable calling of bridging the rather rarified, jazzy New York art world of her father-in-law to that of down-to-earth, down east Maine. She opened a gallery in the home she inherited from Marin, keeping it open some summers.

Joan and Leon Yeaton came to Addison about a dozen years ago and opened Pleasant Bay Llama Keep. In addition to caring for some three dozen llamas, she and Leon have a year-round bed-and-breakfast and a summertime organic farm.

Lobsterwoman Jennie Cirone came to South Addison from closer by, off Nash Island, where her father was a lighthouse keeper. She came to South Addison for love: her husband lived there, but her heart was always drawn to the sea.

DINO FONDA

These people have dreams. Dino Fonda has a mission. The first step was moving to Maine, which Fonda, a retired engineer, did with his wife in 1987. The second step is the building of the boat. The third step will come in about two years, when the boat is finished and the couple and a chosen crew will sail the globe in the name of peace.

Like the ship Fonda is building, which relies on both the strength of its construction and the motion of the water, Fonda's mission is a twining of practicality and faith. A lifetime of engineering experience ensures the boat's seaworthiness; its future he places in the swells of Providence. He's not quite certain how the vessel will promote peace or brotherhood, but he trusts the way will open up. Nor does he fully understand why he came to Maine.

"I wanted to build a boat," this soft-spoken man says. "I believe I was led by Providence to do it here. We want to sail around the world in the name of brotherhood, peace, and prosperity. My wife, Catherine, and I are committed to it." Press him on details, and he'll speak of taking youths on learning voyages, but nothing is certain: "The way will open up," he adds. He does not question further.

Dino was raised Catholic, the son of a sailor from the North Adriatic port of Pyrano. His father jumped ship in the

United States and raised his family in Philadelphia. "All my people on my father's side were shipbuilders, seamen," says Dino. "Even my name, Fonda, means someone who makes anchors. I have twenty-one paintings my father painted, all are seascapes. Boats were enculturated in me."

The future shipbuilder went into mechanical and electronic engineering, creating environmental chambers for the space industry and consulting on vaccination machinery for the pharmaceutical industry. Boatbuilding was a hobby remembered later, when he built a few dozen pleasure boats. "I built them and then sold them. They didn't take long."

In the mid-1980s, after living a life he describes as, "not bad, just selfish," Dino was diagnosed with chronic leukemia and asbestosis. That same year he cut a tendon in his thumb so deeply that he was told it would never work again.

"I knew it was time to seek the truth," he says.

Eschewing medical treatment, he hauled out a copy of the Old Testament and began studying. Today, his lungs are clear, his blood healthy, and though there is scarring on his thumb and the nail is gone, his hands do a fine job of holding a hammer, fixing an engine, and, clearly, building a ship. As he gestures over at his boat, a small smile creeps onto his lips. "I have a private joke with myself," he says. "I don't know what I want to be when I grow up."

Dino started shaving timbers on his schooner on January 1, 1991. He laid the keel during the first week of April. What with winter and pickup jobs, he's only been able to work on the boat about 50 percent of the time. "I'm here longer than I thought I'd be," he says, with a hint of apology. His wife brings home the steady pay, teaching Spanish at a high school due west in Sullivan. They live in the trailer they pulled behind them on their way up from Florida.

Deftly, Dino climbs the weathered wooden scaffolding that leads to the plywood deck. Though the ribs are still skeletal, most of the decking can be walked. He's relying on late nineteenth-century construction methods like iron fastenings and double planking (the hull will ultimately be three inches thick), but adding some twentieth-century safeguards. Among these are a plastic cement sealing compound and pressure-treated pine plywood decking, which will probably be fiberglassed.

The design of the ship is typical of vessels that would have been constructed in the late 1700s in the Mediterranean. It has a shallow draft, enabling the large vessel to sail coastal waters, and sail rigging reminiscent of earlier days.

"It will be a gaff-rigged, traditional schooner, having a foremast and a main mast," Dino continues. "We will carry two head sails and a club-footed jib, and may put on top sails. It will displace forty-eight tons and will be certified to carry forty-nine deck passengers." The boat is sixty feet long.

The original called for a still wider stern. In fact, coming upon Dino at the water's edge hammering away by himself at this huge, heavy vessel inevitably conjures images of the ark. This is what Noah looked like, I'm certain, swarthy and friendly, building a huge vessel on faith.

Dino laughs. "No, we don't know anything you don't know. And we don't plan to take animals aboard." But he does have more than a passing interest in the Middle East.

A car honks as Dino talks, and he waves from on high. Looking over the river as it curls among the marshes, thinking of help received from friends and acquaintances, he says, "We've really been blessed."

Like others marching forward with a mission, Dino collects signs that this is where he's meant to be. Some years ago, a local man invited him to his woodlot where there were two trees he had saved from a cutting four years previously. "He said he had the feeling he should keep those two pines; now he knew why," Dino recalls. They were straight, old white pines, seventy feet tall, like those that centuries ago supplied the British fleet with its masts.

Dino takes even an early disaster, the total destruction of his workshop, as a sign. All was lost, he says, except for the items that pertained to the boat.

There's another sign. This one also mixed and just a bit eerie. I had always linked Dino's boat to the sailing of the *Nellie Chapin* from nearby Jonesport. That ship sailed over a century ago, in 1866, led by the missionary, actor, and alcoholic George Adams, who managed to entice 157 families, mostly from Maine, including 100 from Addison itself, to leave their homes and journey to Jerusalem to establish a community in the Holy Land.

Dino, however, knew nothing of that voyage until he drove to Maine, chose Addison for a home, and this particular weed-grown boatyard for his work. It was then he discovered that his would not be the only boat to leave these ways with a mission. His was the yard where the *Nellie Chapin* was built.

In a cemetery on a ridge above the yard, practically on top of Dino's head, rests the builder. And George Adams, who could mesmerize an audience and infuse the settled, notoriously conservative Mainers with the messianic zeal to give up everything for the unknown desert, lies buried not in Maine, but in a family plot in Philadelphia, close to the resting spot of Dino's own ancestors.

Never mind that the Adams mission suffered from numerous deaths, arriving as it did in Palestine at the tail end of a cholera epidemic, or that the man sent ahead to buy land for the group absconded with their money, or that the descendants of those who returned (buying passage with money offered by Samuel Clemens) are still so resentful of Adams that they prefer not to speak of their ancestral shame. Dino relishes the connection. What this Shakespearean actor and sometime alcoholic wanted to establish, says Dino, was something like the first kibbutz—a religious community devoted to farming, opening the way for more believers to come to the Holy Land.

LLAMA KEEP

Down the road from Dino, on the west edge of Pleasant Bay, past a sentry of an old mobile home with vintage turquoise and white stripes on one side of the road and a small 1835 cape on the other, stands the Pleasant Bay Bed & Breakfast Llama Keep.

Joan Yeaton, the outgoing, friendly proprietor, greets me at the door. No, she says, she is not from Addison, but she is from the region. Raised in Machiasport, she lived for years in Exeter, New Hampshire, where she and her husband raised six children. Her interest in llamas stems from before her family days, however, when she worked in a joint YMCA and Peace Corps project in the Andes Mountains of Venezuela and Peru.

"When my children were grown, I looked around and wondered, 'Well, now what will we do?' And then I said to my husband, 'We can always get a couple of llamas.' I was joking, of course."

Lo and behold, there came an anniversary, and with it, a couple of llamas. Joan's llamas now share the grounds with an organic farm in which she and Leon raise much of the food they need for the bed-and-breakfast. She has chickens, which she enjoys squawking at, and goats. What she can't raise, she is frequently able to barter. "We swap vegetables for chickens, potatoes for fish. We even swapped manure for scallops—that's got to be the all-time best deal."

But llamas take center stage. Even inside their home, llamas are everywhere—little Andean doll llamas perched on

windowsills, photos of llamas on the wall, not to
mention the llamas by the dozen in several
pastures in front of their home, which is brand-
new but created in the style of old New England
farmhouses, with rambling rooms and wide
floorboards.

"Llamas are by far the easiest, gentlest, most
intelligent, clean animals," enthuses Joan. "Their
brains are one-third again larger than a horse, but they are
smaller than a horse, so they are very smart. Our guests love
them."

So does Joan. She may be cheerful and friendly to her
guests, but her love is reserved for her llamas. She chirps and
coos at them, calls them each by name, nuzzles and strokes
them. The Yeatons breed their llamas, selling most of the
offspring. People buy them for pets, for "wool" (but it's not
wool, it is fiber, which is hollow-cored, warmer than wool,
and has no lanolin to upset the sinuses of those with aller-
gies). They also buy them as hiking companions (guests are
free to pack a llama for a day hike) and as guard pets.

"People buy llamas to protect sheep and goats and deer.
They protect their territory. They are very old, primordial
beings with strong herding instincts. They seem to have the
predator profile embedded in their brains, and if one attacks,
they spit and stomp. It's almost 100 percent effective. Even
coyotes don't like getting spit on."

The animals gestate for almost a year. Those that breed in
spring give birth in spring and those that breed in fall give
birth in fall. When I visited one early fall, I found five
enchanting stick-legged newborns. They had been born the
day before, right in front of a few lucky guests.

"It's fun when you see that kind of joy in people's faces.
Gets people back to the basics on their vacation," says Joan.

And that's the point of a vacation in one of the three
rooms of Pleasant Bay. You can drive around and visit the

region, accompany a lobster boat, marvel at Columbia Falls' Ruggles House and the several craft shops nearby, or you can stay put, walk to the beach, take a hike, or simply cuddle a llama.

Even if you don't plan to stay at the "keep," stop by to say hello to the llamas. While you're there, you might want to pick up some organic vegetables at the farmstand.

ADDISON TODAY

Addison may be less of a dream for those who have always lived here. The 1960s and '70s were difficult for rural Maine. Addison's population plummeted to 744 in 1960, though it has risen steadily in the 1990s. The economy is still shaky, however. While one-quarter of the households in Maine earn less than $15,000, 42 percent of Addison households earn less than that; the median household income is only $17,000 a year. (That's a greater amount than nearby Jonesport, but less than Washington County as a whole.)

It was the decline of the maritime life, beginning with the introduction of the railroad, that changed Addison and most of down east Maine, so much so that Washington County has surpassed Waldo County as the poorest county in the state (Waldo Country lost its poultry industry about twenty-five years ago, but since gained a major credit card company).

As in many Maine towns, Addison has experienced a roller-coaster cycle of industry and loss over the decades. Today's fishing folk, clammers, and seasonal forest and agricultural workers are equaled in numbers by service and managerial or professional workers, but the general sense is "a variation on the theme of getting by," as sociologist Louis Ploch of the University of Maine explains it, "through a skillful, and in some cases, ingenious, combination of clamming, lobstering, worming, and wreathing." Lately, the dangerous but profitable business of diving for sea urchins has become another source of regional work. Still, in February, when none of these activities is very promising, unemployment can be 20 percent.

Addison was originally a place of numerous Native American settlements, including those of the Red Paint people. In about 1770, fishermen from Cape Cod and Martha's Vineyard came to the region, attracted by the cod in the waters and the salt marsh hay on land, and developed three settlements—Addison Point, Indian River, and South Addison. In 1860, the population peaked at 1,262, when Addison, like most small Maine towns, kept its population busy with an assortment of industries. Potatoes were grown in the loamy soil, "black diamond" granite and pink feldspar were quarried, spruce forests were harvested and milled, silver was mined, and the water from the Addison mineral spring was bottled. There were manufactories of carriages and sails, and two boatyards produced ships. At that time, Addison may have been less isolated than today, when shipping out on the high seas, and "coasting" or plying the coastal waters, made a cosmopolitan population of Addison's children.

COSMOPOLITAN ADDISON

There's a charming story told by writer Philmore Wass in a 1993 article in *Down East Magazine* about his mother, Mabel Crowley Wass, describing her first journey away from Addison to join her sailor-husband. Mabel was nineteen in 1902, when she married Hervey Wass, a ship's engineer. He shipped off again soon after the wedding to travel down the Gulf Coast to Mexico, promising to return for Christmas. As the time drew closer, however, it appeared that he wouldn't be able to join his young bride. Instead, he sent Mabel a ticket to meet him in Boston, where he would be on duty with the ship. Wass writes the story as his mother told it, in first person:

> You can't imagine how excited and scared I was. I was going to Boston to be with Hervey for Christmas—I, who had never been more than a few miles away from home. I'd never even seen a train. I had heard that Boston was a big place; suppose I got lost?
>
> Suppose I couldn't find Hervey when I got to the train station? And how could I go in my workaday clothes? Life in Addison did not require fancy dresses, certainly none like those the Boston ladies were sure to be wearing. People would turn and stare at me, wondering where such a country bumpkin had come from.
>
> Word quickly got around town about my trip and neighborly offers of help came pouring in. One man who owned a fine horse and sleigh offered to take me to the train station in nearby Columbia Falls. Others were experienced travelers who looked up the train schedule for me and described what it was like to ride on a train. Best of all, one of our wealthier neighbors, who had often visited Boston with her husband, offered to loan me not only a suitcase but some traveling clothes.
>
> Soon we heard sleigh bells jingling in the driveway and I bundled into my warm coat, wrapping a fine wool scarf around my face. All twelve of my younger brothers and sisters gathered in the kitchen, all as excited as I was and all of them wanting to hug me. . . . We tucked ourselves into the sleigh under a big buffalo robe, our feet resting on heated soapstones wrapped in clothes. As I turned to wave good-bye, I remember that everyone was smiling but also wiping their eyes.

For several miles, there seemed to be a well-wisher in every doorway of every house we passed, waving and shouting good luck. The news of Mabel Crowley Wass' great adventure, it seemed, had traveled far and wide.

After enduring the train ride ("I had no idea how big a train would be, and I had never seen anything move faster than a horse and wagon,") Mabel arrived in Boston. There, her Addison-born seafaring husband lost no time in showing her the sights.

Yes, he took her shopping, but he also took her to museums, and to a performance of *Way Down East*, set around Addison. "I can't say their down east looked like anything I'd ever seen," she recalled, "but I'll never forget the real live oxen that they brought right onto the stage."

Hervey later gave up the seafaring life to become a lighthouse keeper. He and Mabel raised five children on Libby Island, far from land at the entrance to Machias Bay, and their son Philmore grew up to write about his family's adventures in his book, *Lighthouse in My Life*.

ISLAND SHEEP

Though in 1902 Hervey Wass was a ship's engineer on a five-masted schooner, already shipbuilding down east was winding down. Four years earlier, in 1898, the last boat had been slipped off the ways and into the Pleasant River at the shipyard where Dino Fonda now works. Dino will not mark the centennial of that launching with his own, however. The work on his massive craft is proceeding slowly.

Work with the hands, both on land and sea, seems to dwindle by the years. A generation ago, coastal farmers frequently kept sheep on any offshore islands that had water.

The island sheep are well fed with grass and kelp, relatively safe from predators, and corralled naturally by the shore. Each spring, the owners, with a crew of sweepers to usher or sweep the sheep into a corral, would arrive at the island for a shearing that generally took two days.

As of a few years ago, the only one keeping sheep on the local islands has been Jennie Cirone, raised on Little Nash, one of nine children of lighthouse keeper Captain John Purington and his wife, Ellen. She and her sister each kept a sheep as a pet. Eventually, through gifts and breeding, a herd developed. Cirone also took to the water, setting out lobster traps at age ten, and a full set or "full gang" of 145 by the time she was thirteen. Later, she and her husband, Stanley Cirone, bought Big Nash, as well as some other islands, keeping sheep on all of them. As of 1997, however, she had sold her sheep on Big Nash to a younger friend. She limits her own sheep to those which, for one reason or another, she took home with her. These, she raises in her yard in the village of South Addison.

At eighty-four, despite the aging of her body, Cirone is still living a life of the land and water, hauling lobster traps, shearing sheep, digging potatoes. One crisp and foggy October morning, she listed the tasks ahead of her: "I'm pulling up all my traps tomorrow, then I'll probably be out scalloping. The guy that dives is busy—he's a physician's assistant—so I got to go out when he can. I'll take the lambs off the island the first of November; I have twenty-six lambs out there, and there are about a dozen that were born in July that are too small to winter on the island, so I'll bring them home. I go out scalloping whenever I can, but I have to get my boat on the bank by the fifth of December, because on the sixth I have to be in Bangor to see if they can get my knee operated on."

With one knee replacement already and a hip, as she says, "of steel," Cirone doesn't do much of the physical work. "I play around on my two crutches and let the others do the work," she says.

OFFSHORE

Much of Addison is oriented toward the water, yet as elsewhere in Maine, it's not always easy for the visitor to figure out how to enjoy it. One simple way is to bring some binoculars and watch the marsh, either near where Fonda is building his boat, from the bridge, or by canoe.

Here, wading birds like great blue heron, snowy egret, and glossy ibis have been seen in spring and summer. There are nesting sparrows (sharp-tailed and savannah), and others fly by on migrations. According to *A Birder's Guide to Maine*, migrating birds include semipalmated and black-bellied plovers, greater and lesser yellowlegs, and semipalmated and least sandpipers.

If you have a canoe or a kayak, however, you might enjoy a trip down the Pleasant River, which passes through Columbia Falls and a long stretch of the Addison Marsh before widening into Pleasant Bay.

The upper part of the river has some rapids in spring, otherwise it offers a relatively smooth passage. The Appalachian Mountain Club's *New England Canoeing Guide* begins this trip thirty miles inland from Columbia Falls, at Pleasant River Lake. There's a swamp, that needs carrying through, and a couple of dams. Bring a guidebook.

It's eleven miles from Columbia Falls into the tidal portion of Pleasant River. Between Columbia Falls and Addison, the river snakes back and forth through marshes, a delightful experience, spectacular for birdwatchers, but bring bug protection. Once you get past Addison, the river broadens and takes on the feel of the bay more than the river, but the AMC guide says you can stay in sheltered waters at least until Carrying Place Cove, across the river from the Addison peninsula, in Harrington. If it's a calm day, and you know what you're doing, or if you're equipped and trained with sea kayaks, you can quietly continue to Upper Birch Island, a hill of an island in the middle of Pleasant River that has become a rookery for some eighty herons on the southern shore of the island. A pair of bald eagles have also nested there. But unless you're traveling after August 15, the Nature Conservancy, which owns the island, asks that you respect the nests and neither land nor linger nearby.

JOHN MARIN

The most famous of dreamers who came to Addison was John Marin. Should you be visiting Addison during the summer, ask around to see whether his daughter-in-law, Norma, has reopened her gallery, Cape Split Place. Even if the gallery is not open, you might make a pilgrimage down the peninsula to Cape Split, where John Marin worked during the last years of his life.

Norma Marin never met her father-in-law. Marin came to Addison with his wife and son in 1933, when he was sixty-three, spending about six months of every year there. By the time Marin died, in 1953, the place had become home to his son, John Jr. Norma came to Cape Split in 1955, sharing summers there with her new husband, John Jr., and winters in Cliffside, New Jersey. John Marin, Jr. died in 1986, leaving Norma as the bearer of the Marin legend.

If you should meet her, you will find a kindly woman of fierce will, a staunch supporter of the region, especially of culture and women in the greater Machias area. Her connection to art is personal, touching, protective. The art at her gallery (when it is open) is offered as if the images were her own children whom she is sending out into the world with fear, trepidation, and a sense of necessity. They were made to be seen. Norma has donated a lot of paintings to Maine institutions. In Machias, the University of Maine has a substantial collection of modernist work thanks to the donation of work from Marin's personal collection; the Colby College Museum of Art in Waterville has a small room of Marin's Maine watercolors.

Marin was a modernist, working at the time American artists were searching for an American art. Like Alfred Stieglitz, Georgia O'Keeffe, Arthur Dove, and Maine's own Marsden Hartley, Marin sought to link his work to the nation. He painted America's steel-girded cities as well as its rugged landscape, capturing the fractured energy of wind against ocean and light streaming through city streets. Though he also worked in oil, Marin painted so many water-colors—often four each day—that he is primarily known as a watercolorist. Using such geometric abstractions as diamonds for sunlight and firm, straight lines for the tides, Marin's watercolors seem to be a jazz dance of the environments he loved. He wanted to capture it all—the light, the movement, even the smell. As he wrote once to his friend, the photographer and gallery owner Alfred Stieglitz:

> To bring something of this back—I for one—hope that I may—just a little—that my paint too shall Smell—a little smell—as a minute equivalent to that great—salty smell—out there.

The journey to Cape Split is itself a bit of a wild jazz dance, growing wilder the further down the peninsula—and thus into the ocean—you go. (You drive down the eastern edge of the Addison peninsula, crossing a bridge over the Pleasant River. After less than six miles, you'll get to a prominent grass triangle. Take a right, onto the Split Road. After less than three miles, you'll get to a bridge, then a dirt road. Cape Split Place is the first right.)

Marin's home, at the end of the peninsula's reach, is on a spare, wind-driven coast where sea storms rage against the rocks. The few craggy trees that grow on the distant islands emphasize the desolate beauty. The first time I drove here, the skies turned stormy as I approached the bay, casting a blue-gray light over the purple fireweed and fields of green and brown grass, alternatingly muting and intensifying the colors. The clouds loosened one lone ray upon the sea, a blessing of white light over a distant island, before closing in again. Having read some of Marin's letters and knowing something of his art, I understood the connection between this craggy-looking man, with his thick, wild hair, his intense paintings, and this rocky land. Marin's paintings, like his words and his adopted home, thrive on essences of energy, as is clear from these notes he wrote Stieglitz:

> Big shelving, wonderful rocks, hoary with enormous hanging beards of seaweed, carrying forests of ever-green on their backs. The big tides come in, swift, go out swift. And the winds bring in big waves, they pound the beaches and rocks.

Places to See, Eat, and Stay

Comfrey Corner Farm: (207) 483-6014.

Machias Bay Area Chamber of Commerce: (207) 255-4402.

The Nature Conservancy: (207) 729-5181.

Pleasant Bay Bed & Breakfast Llama Keep: (207) 483-4490.

Ruggles House, Columbia Falls: (207) 483-4637.

8

GREENVILLE'S WALK ON THE WILD SIDE

(STATE ROUTES 15 AND 16)

From the top of Indian Hill, the thirty-mile vista of Moosehead Lake lies before you—a craggy, forested shore wrapping around blue water, shrouding green-capped misty islands. As you stand here, poised between McDonald's and the North Woods, the maps you've been pouring over in hopes of fathoming the activities of Greenville and its lake suddenly become real.

You feel as if you could give a push and simply glide over the lake like a hawk, or a plane—a seaplane, perhaps. And if you visit Greenville on the second week of September, there will be plenty of seaplanes around, scooting down for landings, settling in the lake like oversized ducks, and then spraying tails of water as they push up for takeoffs during the annual International Seaplane Fly-In. So many come that even Moosehead Lake can't handle them all. Those that don't find rest in the water beach up on land, looking not so much like birds as eager dogs waiting for their owners to unleash their powers.

"The best fly-in there is," claims one pilot, who had flown from Nova Scotia for the event, a short hop were it not for the obligatory customs stopover in Bangor. Other pilots, hailing from elsewhere in Canada and New England and as far away as Texas, nod in agreement.

It is odd to see Greenville, population about 1,800, so flooded with people. Most seasons, Greenville is a quiet archway to Moosehead and the great North Woods. It's a small town, but what a backyard!

It was no larger in the summer of 1853, when James Russell Lowell passed through on his way to the Kineo House on Moosehead Lake. In a cheerfully grumpy journal about the trip (he begins with complaints about the eighteen-hour trip by coach from Waterville, seventy-two miles south of the lake), he describes Greenville as "a little village which looks as if it had dripped down from the hills, and settled in the hollow at the foot of the lake."

Greenville didn't grow any larger the next month, either, when Henry David Thoreau followed Lowell to the woods (that was in September of 1853). Thoreau made two trips to Moosehead. The first time he took the steamer, as Lowell did, continuing to the rough rail at Northeast Carry at the end of the lake. From there, baggage and "birch," as canoes were then called, could be portaged two miles to the west branch of the Penobscot River and from there to Chesuncook Lake, part of the great North Woods. When Thoreau returned in 1857, he and his companion and guide canoed the whole way, paddling one day to Kineo and another to the West Branch, making a grand loop down the East Branch back to Bangor for a total voyage of nineteen days. (We think of nineteenth-century travel as leisurely, but nineteen days was the longest Thoreau spent visiting Maine, the other two trips lasted only two weeks.)

The literary explorations of these men have become part of Greenville lore. At the foot of Moosehead Lake, in a pocket park between the Indian Store and the closed restaurant that used to be called Red's, stands a large sign mapping out Thoreau's journey. The central placement of this monument to Thoreau represents Greenville's lure. Much more than a town, Greenville is a longing. Stand at the foot of the lake and you long to take off by canoe, motorboat, seaplane, or at least overlook it from Indian Hill or even from the top of Squaw Mountain, remembering Lowell's words:

> The forest primeval is best seen from the top of a mountain. It then impresses one by its extent, like an Oriental epic. To be in it is nothing, for then an acre is as good as a thousand square miles.

What you see is lake, mountain, cloud, and a forest that does look to be the forest primeval. And though it is not, the rush of the wild still enters.

Perhaps that is why Greenville, after all these years, is still an almost sketchy place, a place that seems as if it were not yet entirely established, or perhaps uncertain of its identity. It's a small town, a collection of Victorian-style homes and some scattered bungalows edging the river. It's a quiet town, and frequently a lonesome town, too, quite far from even a movie theater. There's a wallop of beauty to it, but not much industry except that of North Woods logging and tourism— both of which lead away from town and into the forest.

As Ed Walden, an elderly farmer and direct descendant of the founder of town, once explained, "It's a wonderful place to live. It's a horrible place to make a living."

Indeed, more than any other mountain and lake community in Maine, more than Rangeley, and certainly more than

Bethel, Greenville has a sense of the wild. Greenville is where the forest met the farmer, where the furrier sold his goods and, most obviously, where the lumberjacks came in the weeks between mud season, when work crews could no longer slide logs around on the snow and ice and total ice-out, when crews would be hired again to drive logs downstream to the mills and waterways farther south. The weight of winter pay may have been an even heavier burden than the logs each man skidded from the snowy woods. Descending upon Greenville, they spent part of their salary replacing their lice-ridden clothes, and part on places like the Push and Pull Bar, gone now. Even the brawny outrageousness of the Road Kill Cafe, with its "Bye-Bye Bambi Burger" platters, couldn't approach that lumberjack spirit. (The Road Kill Cafe is also gone, replaced in 1998 by the Frog Rock Cafe.)

Greenville may have a wilderness reputation, but it was actually founded by a group of farmers. In 1825, they divided up the area into lots, put the lots in a hat, and kept pulling and trading until each man had adjoining property.

When time came to think of a name for the town, Cuba was chosen. Perhaps the disparity between tropical paradise and winter wonderland was too great and Greenville (which it is when it's not Whiteville) it became.

Though settled by farmers, Greenville immediately rang with the axes of woodsmen. They did not go far for the winter, sometimes only to Lily Bay. Now it's a state campsite and a central hub, not more than five miles and a drive of ten minutes up the eastern edge of the lake. A hundred years ago, however, it was considered a distant destination—too far to return home from during a winter's labors.

HERMITS OF THE NORTH WOODS

Perhaps the best way to understand the real solitude of the North Woods is by thinking of the hermits who holed up in the north woods, living for years in isolation in the same locale where today woods workers commute to lumbering jobs. The 1937 Works Project Administration guide to Maine, *Maine: A Guide Downeast*, describes a few.

There was Angus McLean "and his nameless partner, on Indian Pond." They "never spoke to each other, nor would they acknowledge one another's presence before a visiting warden." Another was named Ernest Hemingway. He was not the novelist, but was a top musician traveling with John Philip Sousa's band, "until he was crossed in love and took to the woods." And there was Hiram Johnson, who floated scrap iron on a raft twenty-two miles down the west branch of the Penobscot River to sell it. He didn't like the price, so he poled the iron upstream to his camp at Chesuncook— then sank it. Johnson burned to death in his camp after shooting a man.

Not all were mean-spirited. Joe Klimchook was a calvary officer in the Imperial Russian Army before bowing out of society, moving to Russell Stream near Pittston, about one hundred miles north of Greenville. He just wanted to be alone. Others simply preferred animals. Jim Clarkson was "a powerful man with a flaming red beard, sole resident of Township 9, Range 14, who never shot a deer, but kept many as pets, calling each by name." He spent some time tending Locke Dam, between Chamberlain and Eagle Lakes, now a part of the Allagash Wilderness Waterway. (The waterway began as a dammed river system, reversing the flow of the rivers so river drivers could push logs downstream toward Moosehead Lake and eventually down the Kennebec River.) Clarkson was a beloved man. When he turned eighty, war-

dens by the plane- and canoe-full came to celebrate. Upon
his death two years later, Bangor Hydro-Electric Company
established a fund in his memory.

This frontier, once a solace to the unsociable, is quite
accessible now. It's a managed wilderness, what some call the
"paper plantation." Where hermits once lived and explorers
disappeared for a month or more at a time is now an afternoon's drive on dirt roads. Where logs once cascaded down
rapids, inflatable rafts now take visitors by the busload.

Woods once dotted with logging camps are filled with
roads that lead easily to trails, secluded lakes, and overlook
ridges too numerous to name. But when Thoreau visited the
North Woods, the territory was still being felt out. On his
first trip to Moosehead, Thoreau encountered some explorers whose work caught his fancy, as if they were the distilla-
tion of his romance of the woods quite in themselves. In his
book *The Maine Woods*, he writes:

> I have often wished since that I was with them. They
> search for timber over a given section, climbing hills
> and often high trees to look off, explore the streams by
> which it is to be driven, and the like, spend five or six
> weeks in the woods, they two alone, a hundred miles or
> more from any town, roaming about and sleeping on
> the ground where night overtakes them, depending
> chiefly on the provisions they carry with them, though
> they do not decline what game they come across; and
> then in the fall they return and make report to their
> employers, determining the number of teams that will
> be required the following winter. . . . It is a solitary and
> adventurous life, and comes nearest to that of the trap-
> per of the west, perhaps. Working ever with a gun as
> well as an axe, letting their beards grow, without neigh-
> bors, not on an open plain, but far within a wilderness.

Later on in his account, however, Thoreau grows more

attached to the thing hunted—the white pine—and scorns the hunters.

Strange that so few ever come to the woods to see how the pine lives and grows and spires, lifting its ever-green arms to the light—to see its perfect success, but most are content to behold it in the shape of many broad boards brought to market, and deem that its true success! But the pine is no more lumber than a man is, and to be made into boards and houses is no more its true and highest use than the truest use of a man is to be cut down and made into manure. There is a higher law affecting our relation to pines as well as to men. A pine cut down, a dead pine, is no more a pine than a dead human carcass is a man.

MANAGED WILDERNESS

Thoreau had feared that Moosehead would change by becoming cleared all along its banks, but though there are some habitations farther up the lake, including the half-million-dollar estate that once belonged to child psychologist Lee Salk (brother to Jonas of polio vaccine fame), for the most part Moosehead's edges have not been cleared. By law, a fringe of forest must remain around all Maine waterways. Inland, however, the effects of logging are obvious. This is a wilderness divided among the state's paper companies but primarily owned by S. D. Warren. The companies hire log-gers to take down whole forests at a time for use mostly in the paper industry, but also for construction, burning, and other purposes. Since the 1980s, clearcuts have been the dominant means of harvesting, producing an odd patchwork in the great expanse of woods. You'll drive miles down a dirt road and then come upon a section of torn-up soil denuded of all but a few slender birch trees smaller than a woman's wrist. One spot will have weathered brush piled by the road; nearby there will be a large row of straight, narrow poles, stacked and waiting. Then you'll drive past woods again, and soon past what looks to be a Christmas tree farm.  This is the forest replanted, but only the quick-maturing, softwood evergreens rise through the brush because a herbicide is used to suppress the hardwoods.

Keep driving and the woods will thicken again and you'll arrive at a silent lake ringed by mountains. Although you have passed several pickup trucks barreling down the roads, you alone have come to paddle this lake. A couple of slate-colored juncos will fly close to the water, then flit near your canoe, checking out their visitor, and then zigzag their way back to the woods. A loon will call out mournfully, and you'll be amazed that such silence and remove even exists. Then you'll look up to find the hill beyond is shorn to its boulders, so it looks not like the woods at all, but rather a coastal blueberry barren, or an Alpine peak, too high to bear trees. And you'll remember this isn't a wilderness at all, but a paper plantation, that unsettling mix in which miles of what appears to be the forest primeval is actually some company's farm; it belongs to them, and you and the small moose family you just passed are on the land at their grace. These plantations are so large, their environments so complex, that the philosophy surrounding the appropriateness of their use is also quite complicated.

But even when Thoreau and Lowell came to Moosehead, the wilderness was already becoming managed. The two writers, after all, took steamers up the lake. And Lowell stopped not beneath boughs on the shores of Moosehead, but at Kineo House, on a peninsula dangling into the eastern curve of Moosehead Lake known as Mt. Kineo.

KINEO

Located about two-thirds of the way up Moosehead, Kineo is a large rock or hill at the end of a very large peninsula that swoops down into Moosehead Lake from the east. This peninsula is so large that Moosehead, which can be twelve miles wide, here narrows to only five-eighths of a mile. On the peninsula, towering above the lake, is a seven-hundred-foot stone cliff made of rhyolite, a fine-grained igneous rock. Just as the woods surrounding Kineo are today a source for our homes and paper, five thousand years ago, Mt. Kineo was a source for tools. Kineo's rhyolite was known far and wide among Native Americans for its chipping and edge-holding capacities, all the more desirable because the stone simply flaked off the mountain in large fragments, without having to be mined. Centuries ago, Native Americans came here for trade and manufacture, using the rock for knives, scrapers, and arrowheads. Some even say that the current concave formation of the cliff is not natural, but caused by the chipping away of stone over centuries.

There is not much information on the early populations of the area, but it seems that the Maliseet, who were part of the larger tribe of St. Francis Abenaki, lived here, at times fighting for their claim to the region against the Mohawks who descended upon Kineo from the St. Lawrence River.

While information is sparse, legends about Kineo abound. One speaks of Kineo and what is now called Squaw, Moosehead's other renowned mountain. The warrior Kineo, or Kinneho, a great but quarrelsome man, left his tribe and decided to live on the mountain that bears his name. The lonelier he got, the angrier he felt toward his people. One evening, he looked over the black waters of the lake to see a bright blade of flame on Squaw. He left Kineo at dawn to investigate. Arriving at the summit at dusk, he found the embers of a fire and beside it his exhausted old mother who had come to bring him back to his kinsmen; as she died, she begged him to return. Kineo buried her by the fire and obeyed her request.

Kineo continues to attract mystery and tragedy, as if the warrior Kineo had eventually returned to his hermitage, resentment refocused.

The first Kineo House was built in 1848 and served by the steamers *Amphitrite* and *Moosehead*, which had summer excursions from Greenville to Northeast Carry twice a week. When Lowell came to Kineo House, he stayed five days at three dollars a day including room and board.

But twenty years later that house was destroyed by fire. A second hotel opened, but also burned down. In 1884, a third hotel was built, complete with steam heat, elevators, bathrooms, telegraph, post office—and fire escapes. It offered a four-hundred-seat dining hall and orchestra performances, attracting visitors from Philadelphia, New York, and Boston who came by rail to Greenville, then transferred to the steamer. By leaving Boston at 10 A.M., you could arrive in Greenville at 7:50 P.M.

Today there is no longer a grand hotel. While the building was being demolished, yet another fire (which some call suspicious) completed the job, leaving a lonely annex. It was recently offered for sale, but with no takers. In 1995, the owners upped the ante, offering it for free to anyone with the estimated $1 million to cover repairs. But even $1 million was too low an estimate. Again, there were no takers. By 1996, all hopes of rekindling the era of such leisurely, elegant resorts were abandoned, and the annex, too, was torn down.

The cliffs at Kineo are now public reserve land. Below them, where the resort once stood, there are plans to renovate the old servants' quarters at Kineo into motel rooms, turning the old breakwater house into suites, augmenting the only lodging left on the peninsula, the six-room Kineo House

Inn, famous for its lunches. According to owner Marshall Peterson, the activities at Kineo are still relatively the same as they once were, but without the orchestra. Though people no longer come with nannies and servants and great trunks filled with morning jackets and evening wear, they do settle down for a weekend or a week to swim, boat, fish, hike, snowmobile, explore the North Woods, and dodge golf balls. Kineo is still known for its golf course, which is open to visitors but remains an odd contrast to the primal mountain of rock hovering above.

To get to Kineo when the ice is on the lake, you can actually walk, ski, or snowmobile across from Rockwood, on the western shore of Moosehead. Other times, you can canoe or take one of the launches that operate from Rockwood. There's also a logging road around back to the peninsula, but a gate stops traffic two miles before the mountain, except in winter. The other way to get to Kineo is the same way Lowell did, by steamship. The *Amphitrite* no longer runs, but the *Katahdin*, built in 1914, is her direct descendant.

TRAVELING MOOSEHEAD

When she was launched, the steel-hulled *Katahdin* was one of a fleet of fifty-five ships that delivered people, supplies, even cattle to the many settlements around the lake during the seven or eight months that Moosehead is ice-free. But when roads were built into the wilderness, life on the lake changed and most of Moosehead's ships were beached. *Katahdin* took on a new life as part of the great river drives, towing huge booms of logs down the lake to East Outlet, where river drivers would send them down the Kennebec River. This elegant

The Katahdin

boat, with its open decks and romantic lines, could tow 6,400 cords in one boom.

The river drives ended in 1975. By 1984, *Katahdin* was refurbished as a tourist boat offering daily excursions of from three to eight hours. The museum at the ticket office recalls Greenville's past grandeur and *Katahdin*'s past labors.

Before people took steamships around Moosehead, however, canoes were the means of passage. In those pre-engine days, Moosehead was a crossroads of what was known as the Indian Trail, an inland trail of rivers, lakes, and portages that could take one via birch from Penobscot Bay to the Penobscot River as far as Howland, where the Piscataquis River enters, into Sebec Lake to Wilson Stream and lower and upper Wilson Pond. From there, with a long portage to Moosehead Lake, the route would continue to Northeast

Carry, to the West Branch of the Penobscot River, north-ward to St. John and from there into Quebec via the Riviere du Loup.

People in Maine are more familiar with another passage north to Canada, attempted during the Revolutionary War by Benedict Arnold (in his days as a hero, not a traitor). It had disastrous consequences because Arnold took the wrong way, following a more westerly route, up the Kennebec River, resulting in long portages through chest-deep muck with heavy wooden bateaux. It's always important to get good directions, even today. Navigation through the logging roads of the North Woods is possible, but tricky. If you decide to venture into the maze of dirt roads, be sure to carry DeLorme's *The Maine Atlas & Gazetteer*, clock your mileage at each turn, and look out for other signs, like bridges and marshes, to determine your location. As good as DeLorme is, it can't keep up with the multiple new logging roads each season brings.

In winter, snowmobiles run a different maze, through the woods and across the lake, which freezes over sometime in January, with the ice lasting a good four months. When the ice goes in, the lottery goes on, betting on the date that the ice will go out, often as late as early May.

Surrounding the lake are a number of lodges that are famous for their cooking. Pittston Farm, one hundred miles north of Greenville, is known for its abundant home cook-ing; Chesuncook House offers gourmet French food, pre-pared by the native Parisian who joined her husband here over thirty years ago; and the Birches near Rockwood is a favorite because of its good, hearty fare. In Greenville there's the Greenville Inn, offering a glimpse into the elegance of the lumber barons' lives with its polished wood paneling, drapes of floral fabric, and symbolic stained glass tree rising two stories beside the stairwell. Built in 1895 by lumber money, the inn is now celebrated for elegant European cuisine.

Such places are busy throughout the year, slacking off only between seasons. In summer, guests come to fish and boat, swim and hike; in fall they come to hike, fish, and hunt. In winter they come to ski at Squaw Mountain, or cross-country ski through the woods, and to ice fish on the lake. Come spring, there's more fishing and hiking.

Moose

Spring is also the best moose viewing season, and recently Greenville has been making a lot out of the possibilities of seeing these large, odd creatures, so ungainly that there's something human about them. It's not a given, of course, but come May and early June, the moose tend to wander near clearings, including by the sides of many state roads, searching for the green vegetation that comes up around such clearings.

To find a moose later in June, you have to go to them. Seek a quiet pond or bog filled with greenery. With any luck, you'll find moose munching away at the water plants, night or day. The moose are after salt, their sodium having been depleted over the long winter.

Around Moosehead Lake, several outfits send off moose watching safaris. Dan Legere, owner of Maine Guide Fly Shop and Guide Service in Greenville, says that two favorite spots are West Shirley Bog and Ira Bog, due west of here, off Shirley Mills. (You can get there by going straight on the main road, States 15 and 6, and then making a right turn. West Shirley Bog is directly west of Shirley Mills, Ira Bog directly north up the old Squaw Mountain Road.) But don't feel limited to these; there are dozens of other small trout ponds well stocked with the lilies and other water plants that moose love to munch.

Recently Greenville has given the otherwise slack months of May and June the title of "Moosemainea," offering events like dawn and dusk moose safaris. Offerings vary from year to year, but such activities as a Tour de Moose bike race, a Moosterpiece craft fair, Mooseantics for kids and a Moose Auction—known as an annual black fly affair—are featured. The Moosescapade Parade, led by the town's moose mascot, is getting as big as the Fourth of July Parade, which stretches from Indian Hill through Greenville to junction wharf.

Though moose meat is served at some functions, the celebration is generally of the animal, not its flesh. Moose hunting season, the first full week in October, reverses the reverence entirely. I've heard of moose heads lined up by the dozen, tongues lolling out.

Alive, however, moose are amazing animals. Watch a moose quietly munching on lilies: so huge, yet so calm, as if it were an ancient philosopher mulling over the world, absolutely endearing in its awkwardness. "The moose is singularly grotesque and awkward to look at," Thoreau wrote of the animal in *The Maine Woods*. "Why should it stand so high at the shoulders? Why have so long a head? Why have no tail to speak of?"

Thoreau records a legend relating moose to whale, told to him by Governor Neptune of the Penobscot Indians:

> The Governor said, that "he could remember when the moose were much larger; that they did not use to be in the woods, but came out of the water, as all deer did. Moose was whale once. Away down Merrimack way, a whale came ashore in a shallow bay. Sea went out and left him, and he came up on land a moose. What made

them know he was a whale was, that at first, before he
began to run in bushes, he had no bowels inside but . . .
jelly-fish."

When he came to Moosehead Lake the first time, Thoreau's
companion was seeking to hunt a moose. Thoreau placed
himself as a reporter, not hunting, but curious to see how it
was done. Later, having witnessed the slaughter, he regrets
even that degree of involvement, though he didn't mind tast-
ing its meat:

> But this hunting of the moose merely for the satis-
> faction of killing him—not even for the sake of his
> hide, without making any extraordinary exertion or
> running any risk yourself, is too much like going out by
> night to some woodside pasture and shooting your
> neighbor's horses. These are God's own horses, poor
> timid creatures that will run fast enough as soon as they
> smell you, though they are nine feet high.

Today these moose no longer run from the hunter. Accustomed to humans, they stand to be shot as if they had
become managed wildlife. Which isn't to say that humans in
the woods no longer have a need for wilderness skills and an
ability to read the weather. Should you be boating or swimming, don't venture away from Moosehead's shores unless
you're sure of yourself. Taking a canoe onto Moosehead
Lake, with its temperamental winds and weather, requires
some skill, as does landing a plane onto it.

At the September Fly-In, it's possible to watch hundreds
of landings, as pilots pair off one against the other for the
takeoff and spot landing contests. Some early seaplanes were
fabric-covered and weighed only 750 pounds. "It's mostly a
matter of design," explained Roger Currier, of the contests.
"But there is also some pilot skill," he adds.

That feeling was echoed by a pilot who I found in hip waders deep in the water, checking on a friend's plane. He had let his buddy use his own plane, hours ago, he said in amazement. And his friend was still in the running (winners of each pair get to keep pairing off until they lose). Why wasn't his buddy using his own plane? "Mine is a faster plane," the pilot said, shyly, as if too modest to answer. But why wasn't he piloting it? "Oh," he said, smiling and shaking his head, "I'm no good at that kind of thing."

The friendly competitions continue all day. "Bomb" drops of water balloons onto the lake are another favorite contest. Between contests, Max Folsom, owner of Folsom's Air Service, swooped around with a DC-3 floatplane, the largest floatplane made. The plane is not practical for small lakes, but Moosehead Lake is large enough to land it on.

Soon our particular party headed from the fly-in to the Road Kill Cafe, where we let ourselves be served among the prerecorded screams of animals. While gazing across Moosehead Lake, shadowed by the great North Woods, the source of Thoreau's communion with the wilderness, we feasted on mooseballs, nightcrawlers, and ice water tinted to look like Tidy Bowl. Then we went out exploring ourselves.

Not far from the Road Kill (now equally as bizarre as the Frog Rock Cafe), on the road leading to the ski resort of Squaw Mountain, we discovered a valley trail to a pair of lakes, Big and Little Squaw ponds. It was the perfect hike for a child who finds mountains somewhat daunting. With our son Daniel taking the lead, we made our way through slabs of granite within this moist, luminous forest, crossing over a dam that probably once ruled someone's mill pond, to the lonely, distant-seeming lake. We weren't five miles from Greenville, but we could all be explorers, hunters of white pine, huge moose, or new territory. There was not a soul in sight, not a sound but that of a tiny mouse chasing up a log, a lone loon, and suddenly, the distant sound of thunder. As we returned, our son collected gifts for us: autumn leaves, special stones, sticks. "The best place I've ever been," he crowed.

Places to See, Eat, and Stay

Auntie M's Restaurant: (207) 695-2238.

The Birches, Rockwood: (207) 534-7305, (207) 534-2241, or (800) 825-WILD.

Chesuncook Lake House, Chesuncook: call at Currier's Flying Service.

Currier's Flying Service: (207) 695-2778 or (207) 695-5330.

Evelth-Crafts-Sheridan House: (207) 695-2992.

Folsom's Air Service: (207) 695-2821.

Frog Rock Cafe: (207) 695-8998.

Greenville Inn: (207) 695-2206 or (888) 695-6000.

Indian Hill Trading Post: (207) 695-3376.

The Indian Store: (207) 695-3348.

Jack's Flying Service: (207) 695-3020.

Kineo House Inn, Kineo: (207) 534-8812.

Lily Bay State Park: (207) 695-2700.

The Lodge at Moosehead: (207) 695-4400.

Maine Fly Shop and Guide Service: (207) 695-2266.

Maine Street Station, Moose Safaris: (207) 695-2375.

Moosehead Lake Houseboat Vacations, Rockwood: (207) 695-3494.

Moosehead Lake Region Chamber of Commerce: (207) 695-2702.

Moosehead Marine Museum (SS *Katahdin*): (207) 695-2716.

Moose Safaris: (207) 695-2375.

Mount Kineo Golf Course: (207) 695-2229.

Northern Pride Lodge: (207) 695-2890.

Pittston Farm (call Folsom's Air Service): (207) 695-2821.

Shaw Library: (207) 695-3579.

Squaw Mountain: (207) 695-1000.

9
New Sweden
Takes On Its Past

On a sun-drenched hillside in northern Aroostook County, two little girls somberly march through a community gathering. Dressed in red and yellow calico skirts, kerchiefs at their necks and flowers ringing their hair, each girl gingerly holds a white apron filled with tiny pine cones.

"Take only one," says the larger of the two girls, speaking with the immense authority of her four years.

Around them wander other girls, similarly dressed in calico and flowers, along with a host of friends and relatives who have gathered to watch New Sweden's annual Midsommar festival. This is the festival of the solstice, a day of great meaning to the ancestors of this compact Swedish colony in northern Maine. In Sweden, the solstice is a day without end, a day so long that the sun never sets. This celebration of light and life is a longed-for compensation for the winter days, when the sun lies buried with the earth.

In New Sweden, the longest day is not quite as unending as in the motherland, but the day does mark the beginning of an extended journey, taken in 1870, when the first Swedish settlers left home for the northern Maine wilderness. It also marks a celebration of a stubborn people who have kept their traditions together, giving this seven-hundred-person hamlet the distinction of having the longest-running Midsommar observance in the United States.

POPULATING THE NORTH

It was at the Midsommar Eve festival of 1870 that the first residents of New Sweden took their leave of friends and family, embarking the next day for Maine. The original New Sweden community was an intentional one, organized with the help of William Widgery Thomas, Jr., a Portland man sent by Abraham Lincoln to Sweden in 1863 to serve as consul and keep the Swedes from selling iron to the Confederacy.

When Thomas got to Sweden, says one New Sweden resident, "he fell in love with the Swedes. He married Swedes," she continues, "both of them." (This resident prefers to remain anonymous; we'll call her Ina Johnson.) "Thomas married a Swedish countess," Johnson explains. "When she died, he married her sister."

In Sweden, Thomas perceived some global inequities. Sweden was land poor at the time and only the eldest son had hopes of inheriting land. Maine was land rich but population poor. Thousands of Mainers had journeyed west after the Civil War, hoping to find better soil than the rocky Maine earth, and a climate less severe. The population decrease in Aroostook County was getting to be worrisome, because the County had recently been the subject of a dispute with the British in Canada, known as the Aroostook War. It never did become a war—it looked instead more like a series of late 1830s barroom brawls—but the dispute over the boundary between Canada and the County was quite serious. Much further south, the folks near Bucksport, on the mouth of the Penobscot River, have this "war" to thank for the grand earthworks and granite Fort Knox, perched like a medieval fortress on a hill overlooking the river. In the aftermath of this trouble, it didn't look good to have Aroostook depopulated.

Believing the Swedes to be a stalwart, industrious people needing but a bit of land to prove it; knowing there were vast tracts of land in northern Maine ripe for settling, Thomas arranged a deal. Thomas would recruit a shipload of handpicked Swedes who would pay their own passage to the United States. In return, Maine would give each family one hundred acres to farm.

"Back in those days there were no settlements up here in Maine. A lot of people had left Maine and gone to other parts where they could earn some money," explains Johnson. "In Sweden, there were landed gentry. It was a lot like it is here now, we all used to have individual farms. Now there are only three or four big concerns growing potatoes."

"And when Papa died," she continued, "the estate went to the oldest son. The rest had to fend for themselves."

Thomas arrived in Sweden on May 10, 1870, and stayed through Midsommar. The very next morning, he and fifty-one migrants set off for the New World.

Life was not going to be easy. Trunks were overflowing with all the food the families would need for the month-long voyage, with cloth-ing, linens, and all the tools and supplies needed to cut through the wilderness.

After the first colony was set-tled, the Swedes kept coming. Within six months, the popu-

lation doubled. Within three years, it reached over six hundred. Eventually, the land deal ended, but still Swedes settled in the region, spilling into Stockholm, Westmanland, Perham, and Woodland.

By 1895, there were over fourteen hundred Swedes living in the interior Aroostook hills. When these regions filled, more Swedes came to settle in Monson, Dover-Foxcroft, and Brownfield, finding work in the busy quarries.

The deep valley of Stockholm, just north of New Sweden, became the site of a thriving mill town with three churches, seven general stores, two railroad stations, shingle and clothespin mills, and quite a large veneer factory. Unlike New Sweden, neighboring Stockholm attracted a variety of settlers, including the French from the St. John river valley and Yankees from further east. The story of these mills can be seen in the Stockholm Historical Society.

"I'm not sure that they were completely aware of how much hardship there was," says Johnson, returning to her thoughts of the early settlers, among whom were her great-grandparents. "They came and cleared their land and built their own homes and made their own furniture. They got discouraged, but they had neighbors from the same area in Sweden. They made out. If they couldn't afford a horse, they settled for an ox and if they couldn't afford that, they hitched a cow up to the plow. "But in some ways they had it lucky. Even though they had to clear the land for their farms, at least there were trees to saw into lumber and burn for wood. The ones that settled in Kansas had no trees."

Today the settlement of New Sweden is recognized as a different sort of experience, "farther back in time, not as developed and a little wilder," is how Christopher Olsson, of Minneapolis, Minnesota, who served as executive director of the Swedish Council of America, described it in relation to other Swedish settlements in North America.

"What makes Maine's colony special," he continues, "is that it was a very deliberate, planned effort to create a colony. Others weren't like that. From a historical standpoint, it's unique."

THE ARRIVAL

When the immigrants arrived in Halifax, Nova Scotia, on July 13, 1870, the group, which Thomas called "my children," still had far to go. They crossed the island by land to St. John, took a steamer to Fredericton and river barges as far as they could. One child, nine months old, died en route. The group was becoming discouraged.

But on July 22, the day of their arrival in Maine, a reception committee came to the border to meet them. Writer Pearl Ashby Tibbetts, in her book *Land Under Heaven*, describes that day, telling how the County people awaited their entry, how they had prepared for days to organize a welcoming dinner, and how they all gathered along the road to the border to catch a glimpse of these folks as they entered the nation from New Brunswick. Wearing shoes of wood, the men with high-waisted trousers and the women with shawls over their heads and rings in their ears, they must have looked like beings from another world. To the settlers, too, this world was also a bit terrifying.

Tibbetts relates how after dinner, a little girl named Hilda—with blue eyes, blonde hair, and frightened countenance—whispered something to her mother, all the while clutching a little straw basket.

Her words were overheard by a Danish man, who had immigrated earlier and could understand the question. He answered her and then told the crowd, " 'The girl asked her mother if all these big woods around here were full of bears, and I told her not to be afraid,' Then they all laughed, and Hilda opened the cover of the basket a few inches and showed them a yellow kitten." Yet another immigrant from Sweden! (You can find this excerpt in *White Pine and Blue Water*, by Henry Beston.)

They stayed overnight near Fort Fairfield and continued on the next day, arriving about 2:30 P.M. on July 23 in New Sweden. Their wagons stopped almost exactly on the spot where the museum stands today.

HARDSHIP SURMOUNTED

It wasn't long before the piles of Swedish goods lovingly carted from Europe would be augmented by items crafted from the woods that so frightened young Hilda.

"I've got a lot of things my grandfather made in later years," says Johnson. "He would go into the woods, see a branch, or a couple of branches that looked like something, and bring them home and make a bench or a shelf out of them."

And the woods, at least as described by Tibbetts, were quite beautiful. She quotes her husband, who helped clear 125 acres of land and build the six cabins that awaited the newcomers:

> Nowhere could the woods be more lovely. Mile after mile of rolling hardwood ridges covered with a heavy growth of beech, birch, and sugar maple. There is plenty of black growth on the lowlands. Springs are gushing from the crests of the ridges, and the brooks are full of trout. Deer are everywhere, and the partridges are as tame as chickens. The soil is rich and deep, just waiting for the plow.

Obviously Thomas was not wrong in his appraisal of the Swedes. They were industrious. They worked as farmers, blacksmiths, coopers, and tradespeople. They cut down the forest, farmed potatoes, buckwheat, and rye, added garden vegetables, kept cows, sheep, pigs, and hens, made their own furniture and tools, much like any subsistence farmer. They held regular worship services, eventually erecting permanent churches—Baptist, Free Mission, and Lutheran.

They helped build the roads that would eventually connect them to the rest of Maine, receiving one dollar a day which could go to groceries or supplies, according to Johnson. And they worked as farm laborers, picking potatoes and being paid in "peewees" (small potatoes). If times were good, they ate the peewees. If times were bad, they planted them. It is said that most were planted.

Stories abound of hardships surmounted. One morning, Kersti Carlson left her sick husband and hungry children, axe in hand, for the woods. She felled some cedars, sawed them into butts, shaved the butts into shingles and carried them five miles through the woods to the local store. That night, she returned home with medicine and food, having bartered the shingles for the goods.

George J. Varney's 1881 *Gazetteer of the State of Maine* focuses on the success brought by the Swedes' prodigious industriousness. He includes a description of a Swedish house written by M. E. Elwell of the *Portland Transcript*: "It is one of the larger and better class of houses and shows the Swedish style of building to good advantage. It is built of hewn logs, clap-boarded, with the interstices between the logs caulked with moss—a warm and solid building."

Life may not have been easy, but it wasn't all toil. Elwell writes about "a heavy timber swing, built like a merry-go-round, or flying horses, with a seat at each end of the projecting arm."

The New Sweden Historical Museum

New Sweden Today

Today thirty log cabins remain in the region, including the rare, two-story Noak Larsson/George Ostlund log home with its full attic and cellar, which is under restoration. Though many of the original houses are gone, the old farms are known by the orchards and lilacs that live on, lending a pastoral lushness to the New Sweden community, and completing the picture of a European landscape. Another house, the more modest Lindsten Stuga, is already restored, and stands near the New Sweden Historical Museum, open for visitors.

David Anderson, a recent returnee to New Sweden, tells a story about the first residents of this home. "The man was too poor to bring his family over, so he came alone. He worked all year to bring his wife and child over. Finally he had enough money, and a log cabin to house them in. He wrote to his wife and his child, telling them to come over. But his wife wrote back, 'Do you have a kitchen for me?' "

The man worked another year to build the kitchen, and only then did his family arrive. Today, the crisply white embroidered linen laid over a table near the rough-hewn walls speaks eloquently of the struggle to carve not only a living, but a life of grace from the wilderness.

Many of the artifacts—original ones carried from Sweden, along with the rough tools and furniture the immigrants made when they first arrived—can be seen at the New Sweden Historical Society Museum, a few steps from the Lindsten Stuga, and at the historical societies of Stockholm and Woodland on Route 228.

The New Sweden museum is housed in a replica of the old Capitol, site of the community's early church services, where the store and Thomas's apartment were also located.

There's another story, revealing the centrality of history to the New Sweden community. On June 30, 1971, a neighbor saw a building near the museum get struck by lightning at 6:30 A.M. The building burst into flames. Knowing the direction of the wind, it was clear the museum would not survive. A call went out and people came with trucks, tractors, and wagons, working through the morning to empty the museum. Just as the flames engulfed the building, the double sets of front doors were unhitched and preserved.

By June 30, 1974, a replica of the original building was erected, with all the salvaged artifacts inside and the double set of double doors outside.

Soon after the dedication of the new building, other buildings were set aside. Today, this hamlet of only seven hundred people has a wealth of historic sites. Down Station Road, past a large acoustic bowl on a ridge overlooking miles of Aroostook field and forest and just above the Noak Larsson/George Ostlund log home, stands the Lars Noak Blacksmith/Woodworking Shop. The Noak Larsson family came in 1871, with the second wave of immigrants. Eventually, they built the log home where son Lars Noak began his blacksmithing business. Later he moved it across the street to the present location.

Here Eugene Alward, a retiree, heavyset and stooped, volunteers for regular but limited hours. When he's not there, he's close by. A note on the door reads "I can be here in five minutes" and posts his phone number. On a day when the thermometer rose way past ninety degrees, Alward still fans the flames with a double bellows to show visitors what blacksmithing is about. A small group of children gathers around as he twists a narrow iron rod into a hook.

When asked about the shop, Alward smiles. "A lot of us helped restore it," he says, adding, "I do this because it's important, I want it to go on." His pride and joy are the double bellows he repaired. Because the lower bellows lies below floor-level, it was not an easy task. "I came home covered with grease," says Alward with a small smile. "The wife was none too pleased." He speaks slowly, softly, bogged down by the heat. Across his shoulder, even as he works, he carries a cellular phone, a bit of protection in case something happens to him.

MIDSOMMAR

During the heat waves that sweep over the County in summer, you may hardly notice the additional heat of the forge. But visit the cavernous rooms of the historical museum for a comfortingly cool moment. It soon became a favorite destination during a recent, scorching Midsommar Festival. Others stopped at the neighboring gift shop, a large, open space that was once a one-room schoolhouse. At one time, says Johnson, nine such schoolhouses educated the local young. She recalls the long walks to and from school and winter rides in the "school bus," a long sled with a cover on it and a stove inside to keep the children from freezing. Now the school is dotted with the orange and yellow painted crafts of their ancestral land. But most villagers and visitors are absorbed in meeting old friends and watching the long process of decorating the maypole.

The New Sweden maypole is not festooned with ribbons. Instead, the twenty-foot pole is covered with wildflowers. Nor are the poles simply mast-straight. They are hung with two crossbars from which dangle large hoops. As a pair of musicians liven the air with fiddle and guitar, members of the community dip into buckets of wildflowers and tamarack leaves, twining these gifts of field and forest around the pole. Nearby, 150 more friends watch the process while visiting with neighbors and munching on hot dogs, cookies, and homemade ice cream. In the heat, the crowd quickly empties a large, bright yellow McDonald's barrel of fruit punch.

Cameras are everywhere; among them are those belonging to a professional documentary maker who films the day from her perch on the museum roof. On the hillside below, David Anderson smiles broadly, his T-shirt damply clinging to his chest as he makes a spot appearance on a friend's home video. While some friends watch, he announces, "We live up here in the north where we freeze all winter long so we can complain of the heat in summer. We love it."

Gradually, the pole transforms. No longer looking like a naked ship's mast, it has become a fairyland figure grown huge. Swathed with leaves, lupine and daisies, dripping with hoops, surrounded by gaily-dressed children, the maypole turns the gathering from a casual picnic to a proud heritage celebration. Once decorated, the pole is borne on the shoulders of four strong men and raised high in a field. First the children dance around it, then they grab their families and neighbors to join in.

Midsommar among the lush hills of New Sweden is one of a round of three annual Swedish celebrations that lure visitors, many of whom are returning to this northern hamlet to see parents or grandparents, or to connect with stories that have been passed down from immigrant to citizen over the century.

On December 13, community members brave the blowing snow drifts for the lovely Santa Lucia festival of lights, the start of Swedish Christmas celebrations, when a young girl dressed in a gown of white with a crown of white, glowing candles brings light into the darkness. And one month after Midsommar, on July 23, New Sweden frequently celebrates the arrival of its ancestors.

In addition to the festivals, Aroostook's Swedish community has retained other customs. Swedish is still spoken here, its lilting accents hovering over many residents' English. Indeed, linguists have come to New Sweden to hear dialects that in Sweden have been lost over the past century and a quarter. But though the community proudly continues its annual cycle of festivals, to which the public is invited, the members remain very private. It is the community's history they want people to know about, not their individual lives.

After the ceremony on the hill, most of the gathering retires to cooler homes, or the local swimming hole. There is a smorgasbord to be had that evening for those who reserve early enough, and a meatball supper for the rest. And afterwards, a dance in a local community center on Route 161. At the onset of the dance, most of the community sits tight against the wall until a few braver members—many of them under ten years old—swirl around the large hall to a lovely polka tune.

As in any living festival, Midsommar keeps changing. Until the 1970s, the Swedes celebrated with the more familiar style of ribbon-festooned maypole. But research, and a visit of European Swedes, convinced those in New Sweden that the more flowery pole would be more authentic.

As for the pine cones the little girls were distributing on that June afternoon, no one has discovered any ancient origins for them, despite the fact that the venerable Richard Hede, past president of the Maine Swedish Colony (one of the major local historical organizations), spent the day with the small cones tucked throughout his flowing white beard.

Places to See, Eat, and Stay

Midsommar Festival: (207) 896-5509.

New Sweden Historical Museum, open seasonally: (207) 896-3370.

New Sweden Town Office: (207) 896-3306.

Nylander Museum, Caribou, open seasonally: (207) 493-4209.

Caribou Historical Society, Caribou: (207) 498-2556.

Goughan's Farms, Caribou: (207) 496-1731.

Rum Rapids Inn, Route 164, Crouseville: (207) 455-8096.

Stan's Grocery, Route 161, Jemtland.

BIBLIOGRAPHY

Appalachian Mountain Club. *The AMC New England Canoeing Guide: A Guide to the Canoeable Waterways of New England.* Boston: Appalachian Mountain Club, 1965.

Beston, Henry, ed. *White Pine and Blue Water: A State of Maine Reader.* Camden, Maine: Down East Books, 1950.

Bigman, Dan. "Greenville: The Shifting Frontier." *Salt 43* (vol. 11, no. 3), August 1993.

Burr, Caroline. "Summer at Captain Hathorne's." *Down East Magazine*, June 1961.

Caldwell, Bill. "Can This Home Be Saved?" *Portland Sunday Telegram*, June 1, 1969.

Carpenter, Dorothy. Unpublished manuscript, 1996.

Cedarleaf, Rev. Wallace. *New Sweden, Maine: A Noble Experiment.* New Sweden, Maine: New Sweden Historical Society, 1994.

Chabot, Leo L. "Auction at the Olson Farm." *Down East Magazine*, November 1968.

Collins, Jim. "New Sweden, Maine." *Yankee Magazine*, December 1991.

Davis, John D. "When Lobsters Were Two Cents Each." *Down East Magazine*, November 1968.

Doyle, Mary E. *Newfield: Notes from Shady Nook*. Newfield, Maine: Mary E. Doyle, 1994.

Elden, Alfred. "Biddeford Pool Once a Famous Fishing Ground." *Portland Sunday Telegram* and *Sunday Press Herald*, October 14, 1928.

———. "Biddeford Pool Said to Be Place Where First Lobster Was Eaten." *Portland Sunday Telegram*, September 29, 1935.

———. "Biddeford Pool Once Important Fishing Center of Maine Coast." *Portland Sunday Telegram*, March 31, 1940.

Holt, Mable Rogers. "Aborigines at Moosehead Lake" in *Maine Indians in History and Legends*, edited by Maine Writers Research Club. Portland, Maine: Severn, Wylie, and Jewett Co., 1952.

Huber, J. Parker. *The Wildest Country: A Guide to Thoreau's Maine*. Boston: Appalachian Mountain Club, 1981.

Isaacson, Dorris A., ed. *Maine, A Guide Downeast*. Rockland, Maine: Courier-Gazette, 1970.

Hill, Ruth Ann. *Maine Forever: A Guide to Nature Conservancy Preserves in Maine*. Topsham, Maine: Maine Chapter, The Nature Conservancy, 2nd ed., 1989.

Johnson, Laura, "Swedes of Aroostook." *Salt 38* (vol. 10, no. 2), April 1990.

Josselyn, John. *New-England Rarities Discovered: In Birds, Beasts, Fishes, Serpents, and Plants of That Country*. London: 1672.

————. *An Account of Two Voyages to New-England*. London: 1674.

Kimball, Mike. "The Secret of Dilly Beans." *Yankee Magazine*, May 1995.

Land, Leslie. *The 3,000 Mile Garden: An Exchange of Letters on Gardening, Food, and the Good Life*. New York: Viking, 1996.

Libby, Steve. *Newfield, Maine: The First 200 Years*. Newfield, Maine: 1976.

Lowell, James Russell. "A Moosehead Journal." In W. Storrs Lee, *Maine: A Literary Chronicle*. New York: Funk & Wagnalls, 1968.

The Maine Atlas & Gazetteer (20th ed.) Yarmouth, Maine: DeLorme Mapping, 1997.

Martin, Lucy. "Whitefield Facility: Its Co-founder Never Turned Patients Away." *Kennebec Journal*, January 7, 1996.

Marin, John. *John Marin*, edited by Cleve Gray. New York: Holt, Rinehart & Winston, 1977.

Meara, Emmet. "Fales' Store Never Fails." *Bangor Daily News*, September 19, 1996.

Olmstead, Kathryn. "Touching the Beginning: History and Tradition Are Alive in Northern Maine's Swedish Colony." *Echoes*, Summer 1988.

Pierson, Elizabeth Cary, Jan Erik Pierson, and Peter D. Vickery. *A Birder's Guide to the Coast of Maine*. Camden, Maine: Down East Books, 1981.

Phippen, Sanford. *Kitchen Boy.* Nobleboro, Maine: Blackberry Books, 1996.

Ploch, Louis A. *Addison: Its Persistencies and Changes.* Orono, Maine: Maine Agricultural Experiment Station, University of Maine, August 1990.

Rowe, William Hutchinson. *The Maritime History of Maine: Three Centuries of Ship Building & Seafaring.* Gardiner, Maine: Harpswell Press, 1948 (reprinted 1989).

Selfa, Terri. "Jenny: Island Shepherdess." *Salt 25* (vol. 7, no. 1), August 1985.

Smith, Joseph W. *Gleanings from the Sea.* Andover, Mass.: J. W. Smith, 1887. (Reprinted in 1987 by Harding Publishing, Wells, Maine, with a new Introduction by William B. Jordan Jr.)

Taft, Hank, Jan Taft, and Curtis Rindlaub. *A Cruising Guide to the Maine Coast* (3rd ed.). Peaks Island, Maine: Diamond Pass Publishing, 1996.

Thomas, Davis. "Biddeford Pool: One of Maine's Oldest Summer Resorts Keeps One Eye Cocked Carefully on the Past." *Down East Magazine*, July 1989.

Thomas, Eben. *Canoeing Maine #2.* Thorndike, Maine: The Thorndike Press, 1979.

Thoreau, Henry D. *The Maine Woods* (with notes by Dudley C. Lunt). New York: Bramhall House, 1950.

————. *The Illustrated Maine Woods*, edited by Joseph J. Modlenhauer, with photographs from the Gleason Collection. Princeton: Princeton University Press, 1974.

Tibbets, Pearl Ashby. *Land Under Heaven*. Portland, Maine: Falmouth Book House, 1937.

Varney, George J. *A Gazetteer of the State of Maine*. 1881. Reprint. Bowie, Maryland: Heritage Books, 1991.

Vietze, Andrew. "Iron Man of North Whitefield." *Down East Magazine*, November 1993.

Ward, Ellen MacDonald. "Fox Islands Thorofare." *Down East Magazine*, August 1990.

Wass, Philmore. "Spring Ritual on Big Nash." *Down East Magazine*, June 1989.

————. "The Grand Adventure." *Down East Magazine*, December 1993.

————. *Lighthouse in My Life: The Story of a Maine Lightkeeper's Family*. Camden, Maine: Down East Books, 1987.

Welch, Tom. "Despite Land Squabble, 'The Pool' Unchanged." *Portland Press Herald*, August 18, 1975.

————. "Biddeford's Pool Beach: A Materialized Vision." *Portland Press Herald*, July 25, 1979.

INDEX